I0569718

PENGUIN BOOKS

THE ANTI-PROCRASTINATOR

Veronica Llorca-Smith is a public speaker and author. After two decades in senior leadership positions leading large teams in Asia Pacific for world brands such as Apple and Estée Lauder, she founded her own business. Originally from Spain, Veronica has lived in nine countries across Europe, South America, Asia, and the Pacific and speaks six languages fluently, including Chinese. She's also an amateur triathlete and has completed over 100 races, including the World Championships of Half Ironman in Vegas and an Ironman in Western Australia.

Veronica uses her professional experience leading and motivating multicultural teams, as well as her passion for cultures, travelling, and sports, to empower others to unlock their potential in life. Her writing and public speaking gravitate around a growth mindset, self-improvement, and personal development, and her positivity shines through all her work. She's a strong diversity and inclusion advocate and leverages her social media channels to raise awareness and inspire inclusion in organizations and society. In 2023, she was a finalist for the Diversity Lead of The Year Award by Women in IT Asia. She also spoke in the 12th Asian Women in Leadership Summit in Singapore in 2023.

Her books include *The Lemon Tree Mindset*, *Conquering Your Burnout*, and *The Flight Home*, which won the Literary Titan Book Award in 2024. Veronica is a mom of two daughters and lives with her family in Hong Kong.

THE
ANTI-PROCRASTINATOR

How Self-Awareness
Can Change Your Life and
Get You What You Want

Veronica Llorca-Smith

PENGUIN BOOKS

An imprint of Penguin Random House

PENGUIN BOOKS

Penguin Books is an imprint of the Penguin Random House group of
companies whose addresses can be found at global.penguinrandomhouse.com

Published by Penguin Random House SEA Pte Ltd
40 Penjuru Lane, #03-12, Block 2
Singapore 609216

First published in Penguin Books by Penguin Random House SEA 2025

ISBN 9789815233803

Typeset in Garamond by MAP Systems, Bengaluru, India

www.penguin.sg

In the memory of my friend Laura Espinosa, who taught me to enjoy every day as if it were the last.

CONTENTS

MY STORY

'How do you get so much stuff done?'

As someone who juggles writing with public speaking, learning languages, exercising, travelling, and parenting, this is the number one question friends and strangers ask me. In 2023 alone, I wrote over 300 articles on Medium and 400 posts on LinkedIn, published two books and three e-books, created my newsletter, and launched my memoir with a publisher. I also continued learning Mandarin weekly with an online tutor, grew my business as a public speaker, and travelled to seven countries across three continents. I exercised 295 days and ran a total of 2,144 kilometres. This happened while looking after my five- and six-year-olds. This is not to brag. It's my life journal, what I have achieved in one year, 365 days. And you can too.

When people ask me how I do it, they are both awed and disappointed by the simplicity of my answer: It goes down to the thousands of small choices I make every day; choices that work for me because I have learned to know myself, my why, my strengths and my weaknesses, and my triggers, both positive and negative. I know what drives me and what doesn't. I'm aware of my distractions, my emotional zones, and my default mindset. I don't always see my blind spots, but I know I have them, and ask for help to spot them and mitigate them. I'm constantly wondering how I can make the most of the day and maximize our most precious and limited resource: time.

Productivity is misunderstood in society. It's not about programming a human to perform like a machine, doing more, better, and faster, but pausing to understand yourself first so that you can lift your anchors and live a more fulfilling life in alignment with your values and your identity. It starts and ends with you. Anti-procrastination is not a skill—it's a choice. Your choice.

Would my morning routine and my productivity tips to beat procrastination work for you? Probably not. I will share some anti-procrastinators' routines to illustrate my points, but this is not a framework for you to blindly implement and magically get results. Self-awareness is the name of the game.

My vision for this book is for it to be your coach, your guide. A good coach doesn't give you the answers; they ask you the tough questions, and it's up to you to do the thinking and find your answers.

A good coach doesn't tell you where to go; they help you find the direction and course-correct when you are lost, but it's up to you to choose your route and navigate through life.

A good coach doesn't do the hard work and the heavy lifting for you; they equip you with the right tools, and it's up to you to use your life compass, put the sails up, and flex your muscles.

A good coach doesn't teach you; they help you open doors and broaden your horizon so that you can know yourself and become your best ambassador, your most constructive critic, and your most compassionate ally.

This book won't tell you to wake up at 5 a.m.

This book won't tell you to follow the Pomodoro Technique.

This book won't tell you to borrow a proven productivity routine.

This book won't tell you to do something for twenty-one days to build a habit.

This book won't tell you what to do because I don't know you, but you do, and you will hopefully find your answers between the lines by the time you reach the last page. That's my vision and my why for this book.

What this book will show you is the importance of knowing yourself and developing self-awareness. It will ask you thought-provoking questions that only you can answer. It will show you how to look inward and dig deep into yourself and how to zoom out to look at the big picture so that you can understand and assess your environment. It will challenge your thinking because in order to change your behaviour, you must change your mindset first.

It will make you look ahead to know where you are headed and, more importantly, where you want to go because we only get one shot at this mystery called life, so you might as well create something epic, a unique canvas that becomes your legacy.

You will learn to look in the rear window to identify your blind spots and have a 360-degree view of yourself from a place of honesty, transparency, and vulnerability. Throughout the following pages, you will discover strategies to beat procrastination I have learned from successful leaders, writers, athletes, and entrepreneurs. However, you are expected to design your own life manual to go from A to B by sharpening your tools, lifting your anchors, and developing new skills that will help you sail smoothly.

Self-awareness is the most important skill for unlocking personal growth. You can't find a solution if you don't know what you are solving for. If you don't see what's holding you back, you will never be able to move forward. If you don't understand where resistance comes from and what lies underneath the tip of the procrastination iceberg, you will always be paddling against the current. If you don't know what drives you, you will continue to live life moonwalking towards success under the illusion that you are moving forward when, in reality, you are drifting behind.

You will read dozens of books with copy-pasted tips and frameworks to beat procrastination, but this book is different. It doesn't tell you how to get things done, but it opens the door of self-awareness so that you can unlock the rest yourself and open not one but many doors you never knew existed. It will help you unlock your chain of reaction by aligning the different pieces and minimize resistance by understanding where it's coming from and what you need to remove it.

The following pages will help you sharpen a powerful tool for making the most of your day, increasing productivity, minimizing resistance, maximizing results, and reducing the time between intention and action. That tool is called self-awareness.

When I was seven years old, I started to have a flair for business and wanted to earn some money to be able to buy toys in the store next door. Watching Mum do the chores at home every day, I realized we had many plants around the house, around twenty or so, and one day, I had an idea. I decided I was going to launch a micro-business: a plant-watering business! We were living in Spain at the time, and this was pre-Euro. My business was going to have only one customer: Mum, and she would give me a 100-peseta coin every time I watered all the plants at home. When I presented my business plan, Dad giggled, Mum was amused, and I was thrilled to have my first job. On the first day, I took my golden coin with pride after watering all the plants and carefully slid it inside my pink piggy bank. That coin was enough to buy a small bag of candies at the store next door, and I was over the moon.

On the second day, after I came back from school, I told Mum I was going to water the plants again. Determined to earn my second coin, I started to roll up my sleeves when Mum warned me, pointing at the corner of the living room, 'You can't water these plants today; some only need water a couple of times a week.'

I was shocked and devastated and tried to convince her, 'But, Mum, plants need water to live, right? They are thirsty, like us.'

Mum smiled and replied, 'Yes, they are thirsty, but if you give them too much water, they will die. They also need sun, but not too much sun; it's about the right balance.' *The right balance.* Life is always about the right balance. I decided to move on to my new venture but kept Mum's words in the back of my mind.

As I was ideating the content for this book, the story of the plants reminded me that it's critical to know how to bring out the best *in* you in order to create the best *of* you. Just like a plant, each of us needs to find our perfect balance so that we can continue to blossom and grow our branches and our fruits.

In life, we are all farmers. We have our little plot of land, and we decide what to do with it. We have full ownership and responsibility. We can work hard and smart and cultivate a fertile soil that keeps flourishing and giving, or we can sleep under a laurel, enjoy the sunshine, and wait to see what happens. After all, there's always tomorrow! Except there isn't. You are either an actor or a spectator; you are active or passive, nominator or denominator. You decide what type of farmer you want to be and what type of land you want to cultivate. It's you with you or you against you, but you must pick a side. It's either a land of excuses and objections or a land of anti-procrastination and action. If you are not your best promoter, you become your detractor by default. It's about choices and choosing today over tomorrow because there isn't always a tomorrow. The biggest human illusion is to think that there's always more time.

You are the Chief Farmer in your land, and you must learn to regulate yourself and your environment. Does the terrain need more water or does it need more sun? You seek the perfect conditions to make the most of what you have. High effort equals high reward, and you don't get to complain about the crop you didn't collect because of the work you never put in. The grass is not greener elsewhere; the grass is greener where you water it, smartly.

I will invite you to visit the land of anti-procrastination and discover tools and fertilizers that will help you water your land so that it becomes fertile and productive. However, your land is unique, and only you know what it needs. You are familiar with the terrain and the surface. You have a vision that is different from mine. You know whether you want to plant trees or flowers; perhaps you want both. But you also know what lies underneath, the stuff under the surface that others can't see because it's your land, and you are familiar with the conditions, the neighbours, the weather, and the threats. Your land doesn't live in isolation, and the more you understand the environment, the more efficiently you will be able to cultivate it. You can have the most beautiful and resilient plant, but if you choose the wrong spot for it to grow, without the right conditions, it will dry and eventually die. Knowing your surroundings and what you need to thrive is just as important as knowing yourself because you are part of a social ecosystem that has an impact on you every day.

If you want to start doing more and get better results in life, you must water your grass intentionally and nurture a conducive space to make things happen. This is your land, the land of the anti-procrastinator.

1

THE CHAIN OF REACTION

The Chain of Reaction

The best way to illustrate how to build consistency and achieve sustainable results is through a chain of reaction with four moving pieces: your identity, your vision, your actions, and your results. Like a perfectly angled domino, each piece impacts the next and can only move once the previous one has been activated—in the right direction.

Identity: Your life signature

Your identity is a multidimensional concept that encompasses your unique values, beliefs, personality, experiences, emotions, and what matters to you. It's not only who you are but who you aspire to be, the better version of yourself—a caring parent, an adventurer, an inspiring leader, a writer. It's your unapologetic life signature that no one can forge.

Vision: Your life manifesto

Your vision is how you translate your identity in the world, projecting it from abstract to concrete, from intangible to tangible. If your identity is being a great parent, your vision might be to be present, caring, and available for your children. If you aspire to be a great leader, your vision might be to help people grow professionally and personally. If you call yourself an adventurer, your vision might be to explore the world and take risks in life. Your vision embodies your identity; it's your credo, your life manifesto.

Action: Your behaviour

The action is putting the vision in motion, materializing the roadmap, and shaping your identity into specific habits and behaviours. For instance, as a great parent, you might prioritize spending the evenings with your children, helping them with homework, playing board games, and reading a bedtime story. As an adventurer, your vision might translate into travelling to remote locations, having new experiences, and creating lifelong memories. Action paired with consistency helps turn the theory of the vision into reality. It might not be every day, but most days, taking big and small steps in the same direction, building momentum to reinforce the chain.

Results: Your reward

Lastly, for the chain of reaction to work efficiently and sustainably, action must lead to results, some tangible, others intangible. The parent might feel closer to their children and have a tighter relationship. The adventurer might feel a high sense of purpose and achievement at the end of the year because they have lived new experiences instead of watching them on TV. Those outcomes help you remove the pixels that blur your identity and make it sharper, clearer, and real. They reinforce that you are becoming who you aspire to be—a great parent, an inspiring leader, an adventurer . . . an elevated version of yourself. Results validate your actions and are the proof that you are living by your life manifesto. They are the reward for your efforts.

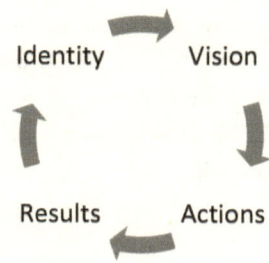

When the pieces of the chain are aligned, they trigger the perfect reaction, a seamless flow, and keeping momentum feels effortless and painless. Once you achieve results, they help reinforce your identity, which strengthens your vision and motivates you to keep going. The virtuous circle carries on, and your chain is in full sync.

This framework can be applied to anything you aspire to be in life: a leader, a writer, an athlete, an entrepreneur, or a life partner. You go from identity to vision and from vision to behaviour, leading to results that validate your actions and reinforce your identity. Like a gentle river following its course . . .

Reflection

Visualize your own chain of reaction, focusing on the new identity you want to embody, and define the four elements that integrate it. For example:

Identity: Being a fit and healthy person.

Vision: Feeling confident about yourself, your appearance, and your health.

Action: Going to the gym three times a week, completing 8,000 steps daily, and eating healthy.

Result: Looking leaner, losing body fat, and being fitter and more energetic.

Resistance

This chain of reaction makes sense and is based on logic. However, humans are not robots wired to perform following a programming code and Cartesian logic. Sometimes, the pieces of the chain derail or get rusted, the domino loses its perfect alignment, and you lose steam. Somewhere between vision and action, momentum is lost, and you stall like a heavy ship in shallow waters. You might give up before taking the first step and quit before trying. It all starts with a good intention, a solid resolution at the beginning of the year, and a genuine promise to others and to yourself, but it doesn't translate in practice. Things break along the way; you deviate from your perfect plan, leaving the chain disjointed and opening an abysm between your identity and the actions you are taking or, more likely, not taking.

Why would this happen?

Why is it so difficult to go from identity and vision to taking the first step and staying committed?

If we are clear on our goals and values, why do we, humans, still procrastinate and sabotage our own identity?

Why do we pull the brakes when we are trying to run towards a better version of ourselves?

Why is there a never-ending echo between intention and action?

Is our chain of reaction broken?

Humans are not a perfect chain in perfect sync. Sometimes, we are not aligned with our values and we feel lost along the way, like when we are chasing money and climbing the corporate ladder until we realize it leads nowhere. Very often, especially in our professional life, our why is not intrinsic and authentic but fuelled by peer pressure, society, or eager parents who want us to become doctors and engineers, even if our dream is to be an actor, launch a business, or do charity work. We are often pulled down by social gravity and reprogrammed to chase a dream someone told us was ours, and when we open our eyes, we look in the mirror and realize that the person we thought we wanted to be is not aligned with our values and our heart. It was never our dream.

Sometimes, we have all the elements of the chain, but we lack a solid plan or the know-how to execute it: We dream a thousand miles above the ground and have a mind-blowing vision but struggle to start off the engine and land the plane. We know where we are and where we want to go, but we can't figure out how to bridge the gap and map out the journey. It's easy to be a dreamer without the doing, and it's also easy to be a doer without a dream. In life, you need both for your loop to be complete.

Yet, most often, something else happens that impacts the chain of reaction and puts it to a halt. Although we have all the moving pieces and the clarity, we press 'pause' and remain where we are, on freeze, unable to take the first step. We have the perfect plan of action, but we delay pressing the start button and setting the engine in motion. Insecurities start to creep in, limiting beliefs take over rational plans, questions take over execution, emotions take over logic—and we give in to procrastination. We delegate tasks to tomorrow we look the other way, avoiding doing things that are good for us, often replacing them with things that aren't. We want to move forward, but we remain still in the same place, adding items to a to-do list that never loses its virginity. We face resistance.

What happens when you push a door that you are supposed to be pulling? You keep pushing and pushing with all your strength, but nothing happens. Two forces fight against each other: the yes against the no, the want against the can't, the courage against the fear, and action against procrastination. It's you against yourself because you are the one incubating that resistance from within, and the sooner you realize it, the sooner you can be in control and eliminate it. The longer you keep going, the harder it is to keep pushing. It becomes mentally and physically exhausting, and eventually, you give up and stay where you are, feeling drained, depleted, and frustrated.

Thinking about the tedious task you have to perform usually creates more anxiety and mental overload than actually completing the task. Feeling negative and apprehensive about submitting the expense report is more mentally taxing than sitting down for thirty minutes and going through the process of reporting and submitting the claims. Postponing an unpleasant conversation or call, such as giving somebody bad news or delivering negative feedback, can be emotionally stressful. The longer we wait to pick up the phone the more pressure and guilt we feel, and we put it off, feeding the false and irrational hope that the task will magically vanish.

Resistance is an invisible burden we create ourselves that holds us back, preventing us from doing, moving, and growing. You must be aware of where it's coming from and mitigate it from within, lifting your fears and limiting beliefs and changing the position of the boat so that you can start sailing with the wind and not against it. Sometimes, you discover that instead of pushing a heavy door, you can actually pull it gently and smoothly without resistance until it finally opens.

Procrastination is simply a manifestation of resistance, and you must deconstruct it to understand it and be able to dissipate it. You decide whether you want to push or pull the heavy door, and the first step is to look in the mirror and have self-awareness.

Reflection

Resistance happens mostly unconsciously: We can't explain why we delay booking an important appointment or why we resist going to the gym even if it's good for us. Reflect on instances of your life where you are facing resistance and identify the feelings they generate.

For example:

I'm avoiding writing a report because it's pointless, and I'm overqualified.

I feel frustrated and annoyed.

I'm delaying writing a book because I'm afraid it won't be good enough.

I don't feel confident.

I'm postponing launching my business because it's overwhelming.

I feel intimidated, scared, and insecure.

I'm reluctant to create my website because I don't know how to get started.

I feel lost and anxious.

I'm struggling to go to the gym because I don't see any results.
I don't feel motivated.

Once you accept the fact that you are experiencing resistance and acknowledge its negative effects, it is only then that you can change it. To understand and neutralize resistance, you must first understand where it's coming from and dissect the emotions behind it.

Your Life Canvas

'One in eight billion, that's how special you are.' I borrowed this line from my first book, *The Lemon Tree Mindset*. Your most precious asset is your identity, who you are as an individual. It's also the rarest asset of all: one in eight billion people. Everybody else is taken, so you better embrace who you are.

Your identity starts with your DNA and encompasses your diversity, both physical and cognitive—what you look like on the outside and the inside, your human expression, and your unique way of thinking. It's your distinctive fingerprint. How you see yourself and project yourself in the world around you determines how others see you. You have the power to shape your own identity, but it starts from within in a space of self-awareness (who you are) and self-determination (who you aspire to be).

It took me many triathlons and sweaty sessions on the bike and on the track to call myself a triathlete, but once I did, I truly embodied it and started to behave like one. I ramped up my training, set bigger goals, and chased them. Telling others that I was a triathlete was empowering, reinforcing, and affirmative. My identity helped to eliminate the resistance and limiting beliefs I had fed myself with. Once I dared to call myself a writer, I stepped into my new shoes. I nurtured the inner strength to reach out to publishers and editorials and began investing in my writing and yielding the dividends of my identity. I started to introduce myself as an author and seek challenges I never thought I would be capable of. I changed the signature I was signing my life with, and by manifesting that I was a writer, loud and clear, I also convinced the world that I was one.

Do you know who you want to be?

Do you know what you want your life canvas to look like?

If not, this is the time to reflect on it: take your brushes, start painting, and find your answer. Once you have your answer, tell the world about it. Shout from the roof that you are an entrepreneur, a doer, a great parent, a public speaker, a writer, a finisher . . .

Paint your canvas one stroke at a time and take pride in the person you become.

Although there is an apparent contradiction between embracing your identity and creating a new one, it's all part of the same journey and the same roots. It's still your essence, but its manifestation is constantly evolving, the same way a bud turns into a flower and a caterpillar becomes a butterfly. Build on the old, grow on the new. Claim your blank canvas and turn it into your life masterpiece. Go in front of the mirror and tell yourself who you are. Reinforce your identity and build your own belief. If you don't believe in yourself, who will?

In James Clear's book *Atomic Habits*, he talks about defining your identity first and creating habits around it: If you call yourself a runner, you adopt the behaviours of such. If you call yourself a good partner, you display the behaviours a good partner exhibits. You are loyal and faithful; you make time for your better half; you are present and caring; and you support the other person's goals and dreams. Your identity shapes your behaviours, and vice versa. As we saw in the chain of reaction, your identity informs your vision, and your vision impacts your actions like a perfect domino in motion. Everything starts with who you are and dream to be.

People who cheat don't usually call themselves cheaters; they tend to refer to the act as an isolated occurrence—'I cheated.' People who lie don't usually say 'I'm a liar'. Instead, they say, 'I lied,' referring to that specific action rather than assuming it as a trait of their personality. When we say we *are* something, we make it part of our identity; we embed it into our DNA. 'I am' carries much more weight than 'I do'. It reflects your moral compass and puts an authenticity stamp on your identity.

How you define yourself has a strong impact on your actions, and you are more likely to demonstrate the behaviours associated with it. When you call yourself a writer, a finisher, or a runner, you are more likely to write, complete things, and run. On the other hand, if you identify yourself as a procrastinator, someone who is always late or terrible at planning, chances are you will continue to procrastinate, arrive late, and plan poorly because you have internalized those behaviours as part of who you are, and you use a self-imposed life bio to justify them, and worse, perpetuate them.

We all have those friends who use their personality to rationalize and normalize negative behaviours. For example:

'I'm always late; it's in my nature.'
'I'm not a planner; I'm terrible at organizing things.'
'I'm lazy; I could never find the discipline to exercise every day.'
'I'm not a romantic; I never have good ideas to surprise my partner.'

By letting those behaviours become our identity, we continue to feed a self-fulfilling prophecy that prevents us from ever being a punctual person, a planner, someone with discipline, or a romantic partner.

Tell me who you are, and I will tell you how you behave.

Tell me how you behave, and I will tell you who you are.

In September 2022, I started my journey as a writer. I published dozens of posts and articles across multiple platforms and decided to take my journey to the next level and write my first book. Writing the book was challenging, but the hardest part was convincing myself that I was a writer and calling myself an author. Saying 'I write' was transactional; it was defined by the action. However, calling myself a writer was a different ball game and carried moral weight, responsibility, and ownership. It meant embracing and owning a new identity and living up to the expectations around it, from others and from myself. It also meant overcoming the imposter syndrome we all face when we are stepping into our new identity shoes. If I was going to call myself a writer, I had to embody it through my actions; I had to have moral alignment, level up my game, and do what a writer does. But in order to do any of that, I had to believe it myself first and evolve my mindset from transactional (I write) to existential (I am a writer). An identity is defined by values, built through actions, and cemented through the mindset: from 'I do' to 'I am'.

I only truly became a writer the day I dared to say four simple words: 'I am a writer.' That's the exact moment I replaced the ID card in my belief system. I updated my profile across my social media platforms and added the word 'author' to all my bios and email signatures. I intentionally changed the language I used to introduce myself: I went from 'It's just for fun' or 'I'm an amateur writer' to saying, 'I'm a writer', 'I'm an author', with confidence. I fully embraced my new identity and owned it, and as a result, the behaviours followed. I continued writing and invested in my brand as an author. My actions consolidated my new identity. I believed, and I became.

When you embrace your identity, others do too. If you project yourself as an entrepreneur, others see you as one; if you tell the world who you are with conviction and act accordingly, the world listens because you shape up your reality. Listening to my new inner voice gave me the confidence to create a new path, and in April 2023, I self-published my first book, *The Lemon Tree Mindset*. A few months later, I approached my distributor in Hong Kong, Bookazine, and asked them the unthinkable: 'Can I do a book signing in your bookstore?' It was the voice of the writer in me speaking, evicting the imposter that had been living there, rent-free, for so long.

As an introvert by nature and an extrovert by nurture, getting myself into unknown situations in public is out of my comfort zone. I do it because I have to, and I want to, but it takes me away from my cosy and peaceful shell. Why did I initiate it? Did I need to put myself under the spotlight? It goes back to my identity. I want to be a writer, a great writer. And what do great writers do? They write, they tell the world they are a writer, they do book signings, and they build their identity around their values and beliefs.

On 19 October 2023, I hosted the book signing in the flagship store in Prince's Building in Hong Kong. I was both nervous and ecstatic, not knowing what to expect. As I approached the bookstore, coming up from the escalator, I had an out-of-body experience. My daughters, Maia and Alba, then five and six, joined me for the special event. They were wearing matching pink dresses and holding hands. 'Mummy, Mummy, look, it's you!' said Alba, who had just learned how to read, pointing at a welcome signage displayed at the entrance of the store with my picture and the image of a lemon tree next to it. 'Meet the author,' she continued, 'that's you, Mummy, my Mummy!'

Wow. That was me, Veronica, the author. Reading those words and, more importantly, hearing them from my own daughter was empowering. I was an author. I am an author! Embracing my new self allowed me to do things I would never have dreamed of before: I approached book fairs, pitched to magazines, and entered book awards. They all had a different outcome: very often a 'no', sometimes a 'maybe', and occasionally a 'yes', but they all had the same signature: 'Writer'.

Once I convinced myself I was a writer, persuading the rest of the world was easy because that's who you are, and that's what you do. In the same way that I don't need to convince people that I'm a Mum, that I'm Spanish, or that I'm married, I don't have to convince anyone that I'm a writer. It's just who I am, and the more I say it and act like one, the more I reinforce it.

In the words of Oprah Winfrey, 'You become what you believe, not what you want or what you think.'

In January 2024, I was approached by the Hong Kong International Literary Fair to be a moderator for one of the sessions featuring a famous Spanish author and poet, Manuel Vilas, winner of multiple prestigious literary awards over several decades. The event organizer contacted me not because of my writing but because of my work as a public speaker and my fluency in English and Spanish; they wanted to host a bilingual session with Manuel. Excited, I accepted the invite, and during the initial call, after a moment of hesitation, I told the programmer, Daniella, that I was an author as well and had just published my third book, *The Flight Home*. I knew they had already filled the quota for the participating authors, and most of them were seasoned writers with some weight and authority in the literary scene.

Deep down, I really wanted to have my own spot, too, but I knew the chances were slim, and I was still busy evicting the stubborn imposter in me. Then, I challenged myself. I wasn't going to waste a precious opportunity, so I decided to tell Daniella that I was an author too and told her briefly about my young writing career. I didn't expect anything in return, but it was a way of vindicating my identity rather than squeezing it into a box of insecurities. Unlike the famous Spanish author, I hadn't won any book awards yet, but I didn't have to in order to be a writer as long as I said it with confidence and authenticity, speaking from the heart.

A few days later, Daniella sent me a follow-up message at 3 p.m. to share some great news. They had been able to secure me a spot at the fair to host an author talk about my new book, followed by a book signing, on top of the moderation session. I was over the moon, feeling both like an Olympian and an imposter. Without knowing any of the details, I immediately accepted the offer. All I knew was that I had an opportunity in front of me to add new colours to my life canvas, and I was not going to miss that shot. 'Great,' she said. 'I need your 100-word talk blurb, author profile, and picture.'

I replied, 'Absolutely. Is tomorrow morning fine?'

'If you want your talk to be featured in the promotional leaflet of the fair, the sooner, the better,' she advised.

She didn't give me a deadline, and she didn't have to. My chain of reaction was already activated, and I did what a writer would do. At 5 p.m., I sent her an email with everything she had requested: my picture, my bio, and a ninety-six-word blurb about a last-minute talk I hadn't planned in front of an audience of strangers in my first book fair. At the time I accepted the invite, I had no idea about the length of the talk, the format, or the number of participants. What if no one showed up? It didn't matter. What I did know for sure was that it was a chance to prove myself; the what and the how were secondary. I would figure things out. All I needed was my why, and I was ready to speak in front of an empty room as much as I was ready to speak in front of a full stadium.

I could have accepted the role of a moderator without telling her that I am an author. She might have dismissed my work and bruised my ego. I could have made myself smaller by saying, 'I'm *just* a small writer.' I could have waited to send her the material until the next day and hoped for the best or waited until she had ironed out the details of my presentation to have more time and be more in control. I could have patiently sat on the procrastination bench and let things flow, see what happens, and watch the show from the spectator seat. But I didn't want a spectator seat, not even a front-row seat. I wanted to be the actor, the author on stage, the woman who grabs the microphone in front of a crowd of strangers about a book she's proud of. I want to be the person who seizes every opportunity and holds on to it as if it were the last, even if that means falling from the heights.

So, I aligned my identity with my vision and my vision with my action. I fought against my own resistance made of fears and insecurities, and I pressed the action button. On 8 March 2024, I participated in my first book fair as an author and delivered my talk with a smile on my face. That was my reward.

When your chain of reaction is in alignment, you don't need a deadline: You make things happen and push the door with all your strength until resistance vanishes and you open a new door.

Exercise

Own your identity. Write down a list of things that you want to define your identity, even if it's only aspirational at this stage. For example:

I am a writer.
I am an entrepreneur.
I am a doer and a finisher.
I am a person with attention to detail.

Think of the signature you want every page of your life to be signed with.

The Power of Language

Language is instrumental in building and reinforcing your identity. How you speak about yourself and the words you use to describe yourself help to consolidate your identity, question it, or negate it altogether. Saying 'I am a writer' was affirmative and empowering.

It vindicated my identity in the outside world through the power of words. However, we often use minimizing language that, instead of reinforcing our identity, diminishes it.

When we use words like 'just' or 'small', we disqualify ourselves before the race has even started: 'I'm just a housewife', 'It's just a side business', 'I'm a small writer'. Even if your business is small or you are in the early stages, you should be proud of it and embrace your identity as an entrepreneur. In the early days of my business, when people asked me about my new business, I used to say, 'It's nothing big', 'It's just me', or 'I'm not really a businesswoman'. By saying those words, I was doing a disservice to myself, discrediting the hard work I was putting into building a new career and living my dream. I was disempowering myself and erasing my life signature.

Growing up, my results in anything related to arts were always mediocre at best. I never received good grades on anything artsy like music, painting, or arts. My parents tried to bring out the Mozart in me by taking me to private piano lessons every week. It only made things worse, and Mozart was nowhere to be found—or heard. I always finished the lesson frustrated and disappointed and ended up convincing myself that I was not creative and wasn't born to do anything or be anything that required creativity. My music professor, Conrado, was equally convinced and frustrated, and it was as much a waste of time for him as it was a waste of money for my parents. I gave up on being creative and assumed a personality trait I carried throughout my adulthood: the non-creative.

As an adult, this limiting belief impaired my work and the way I approached creative tasks. Whenever I was in a meeting and participated in a team-building activity that required drawing, creativity, or any artistic skills, I would be the first to put my hand up and say, 'Not me, I'm not creative.' And I wasn't alone. Most of the time, half of my colleagues raised their hands, too, giggling, 'Same here.' We were the self-proclaimed non-creative bunch. By labelling myself with that tag, I convinced myself that I could never create anything and locked myself inside a suffocating box. I was able to learn quickly, lead large teams, and execute projects, but anything that required creativity was out of my scope and my DNA. As a result, I rejected opportunities before opportunities rejected me.

It turns out that 50 per cent of the room was wrong. By nature, humans are creative. Every single second, our brain processes around eleven million pieces of information, mostly unconsciously, and these turn into thoughts and ideas: creativity. We are constantly ideating, creating, visualizing, and dreaming. If that is not creative, what is?

It was only when I was unemployed, in 2022, that I came to the realization that I was creative too, but I hadn't found the right vehicle to unlock my creativity. I didn't become a singer or start painting overnight, but I found my vehicle in writing. I started to own my creativity and changed my mindset and language around it. I became creative because I started believing that I was creative. I embraced creativity as part of my identity. Today, when people ask me, I nod with confidence and say that I am creative; my vessel of expression is the language of words. I'm still a terrible singer, and I can't play any instrument, but I can create through writing, and my parents don't have to waste any more money on piano lessons.

Creativity is part of your identity, too, and if you say you are creative, you will start to embrace it as part of your nature and find the channels to express it in your own way. Language is a powerful catalyst for reinforcing your identity, but you must use it intentionally. Your words become your reality. If you say you are creative, you are right. However, if you say you are not creative, you are also right.

Who You Don't Want to Be

Knowing who you are, your identity, and who you want to become is a complex question because it's personal, subjective, and intangible, and only you can judge your answer. People spend fortunes trying to figure out who they are. Some go to therapy to reconnect with their inner child, while others go on silent retreats or meditate to unleash their true selves. For generations, philosophers have discussed, debated, and theorized about the why of existence. The answer remains a mystery for most.

Sometimes, it's easier to understand things by defining what they are not, like troubleshooting your computer when it stops responding. It's easier to find out who you are by eliminating who you are not. You might not be entirely sure of who you want to be, but you most certainly know who you don't want to be.

I don't want to be the person who starts living life in retirement. I want to live my best day every day because tomorrow is not a given. Happiness.

I don't want to be the Mum who loses patience with her daughters, lashing out at them due to the stress from work. I want to be a kind and patient Mum who always makes time for her children. Family.

I don't want to see work as a paycheque. I want work to fulfil me with joy and purpose. Fulfilment.

I don't want to live through a screen, missing out on real life. I want to be present, enjoying the moment in the present and the present in the moment. Mindfulness.

I don't want to be the person who dreams about doing. I want to be the person who chases the dream, the runner who endures the miles on the road, the writer who runs marathons on the keyboard, the doer who lives life, and the finisher who crosses the finish line every single time. Purpose.

Understanding who you don't want to be creates clarity: It's easier to see white against black; the night helps you appreciate the day; noise helps you enjoy silence; hunger makes you crave food. Knowing who you don't want to be makes you crave the person you want to be and the values you want to embody.

Finding out who you don't want to be is an exercise of self-awareness and vulnerability because if you are honest with yourself, you realize that very often, you might be turning into the person you don't want to be by default, inaction, lethargy, and procrastination.

Reality check: I have been the person above in the past. For years, I climbed the corporate ladder, flying high, sprinting in the hamster wheel, aiming at targets I couldn't even see. I'm ashamed to confess that after a long day at work, I would be angry at my girls and lose my patience with them, or even worse, delegate the parenting function to an iPad. My favourite day of the month was the day I received my salary, and my ego loved the prestigious title of Senior Director on my business card. Many days, I spent way too many hours in front of a screen, missing out on what was just in front of me: life.

The worst part is not the behaviour itself but the lack of awareness. It's never us; it's always the others. It's other people who spend too much time on social media, the neighbours at the restaurant who behave like zombies in front of their phones, the others who are chasing money, and the others who like to gossip. It's always the others, never us.

The lack of self-awareness prevented me from seeing that I was going through a burnout, with all its consequences: anxiety, stress, sleep deprivation, negative thoughts, loss of self-esteem, and a general sense of apathy. It was only after I left that company and gave up the juicy bonus and the vanity title that I removed my tinted lenses and saw the truth: I had been burning the candle at both ends for over a year and had become a stranger. I had lost my confidence and my sense of purpose, and even months after resigning from that toxic environment, there was still toxicity in my system.

Two years later, once I had healed and thrived out of burnout, I shared my experience openly. I travelled virtually to the dark tunnel and went back in time to analyse my journey, my behaviour, and my decisions. It was so obvious that I was poisoning myself, living in misalignment with my identity, betraying who I really was. The chain of reaction was in motion, but it was fuelled by an identity that wasn't me, and had become a ticking bomb waiting to be detonated. However, at that time, I couldn't see any of that. I was so busy jumping on urgent calls and packing for the next business trip that I forgot to look in the mirror and ask the uncomfortable question, 'Are you happy with the person you are becoming?' Sometimes, you need to take a step back to see the bigger picture—the ugly picture—and act on it.

I thought my life needed to change until I realized that I needed to be the change in my life. That change in perspective was liberating and empowering. If I didn't want to be that person, I didn't have to be that person. I had everything in me: my uniqueness, my values, and my drive to help me create a vision for a new version of myself I would be proud of when I looked in the mirror. I was ready to fill my canvas.

Documenting my experience and process in and out of burnout helped me find clarity. I was able to make sense of the things that didn't seem to have any. My self-reflection helped me connect the dots. It was fine to start my canvas from scratch and give myself permission to paint. Once I saw the light and left the dark tunnel behind, I transformed my journal into a book, *Conquering Your Burnout*. Since then, I have talked on multiple podcasts about mental health and burnout to raise awareness on a topic that still carries a heavy taboo. I use my personal story to advocate for work-life balance and mental and physical well-being. That is the person I want to be, the identity I choose to create, and the values I live by.

Once you open your eyes and look in the mirror with honesty lenses, you become the judge of your actions, and you gain the biggest gift of all: freedom. And with freedom comes the ability to decide who you want to be and the responsibility to act on it.

Knowing who I was not (and who I did not want to be) allowed me to understand my values and who I was and wanted to be: a present and patient Mum, a person with a purpose, a woman who lives life in the moment, and a writer who sees work as fulfilment and not as a means for fulfilment. If you troubleshoot long enough, you end up finding your answer by elimination. The 'no' helps you understand the 'yes' as much as the 'yes' helps you understand the 'no'.

Reflection

Reflect on who you don't want to be, highlighting the behaviours you are trying to avoid. For example:

> I don't want to be the person with a million ideas but who never executes any.
> I don't want to be the person who leaves important tasks for the last minute.

I don't want to be the person who spends an entire life frustrated at work.

I don't want to be the person who doesn't take risks because of fears and insecurities.

By eliminating who you are not, you troubleshoot your identity and start to have clarity on who you want to be and what your life manifesto is.

Finding Your Why

When I had my initial call to discuss this book with my publisher, Nora, I wasn't exactly sure what I wanted to write about. I knew I wanted to use my personal and professional experience and my life challenges and lessons to help and empower others, but I hadn't shaped up the what, the vision, and the message. I wanted to write a book that would make a positive impact on people's lives, but what was that impact?

I realized that I would only be able to have the inspiration to write this book once I went back to the beginning and zoomed out to create a vision, a common thread that would permeate through every single page, through the lines, and in between the lines. What was my vision? What was my why with this book? I started thinking about my friends, my family, and the people close to me. What do they need? What are their challenges? Is there a common theme that travels through cultures, countries, generations, backgrounds, and time?

Then, one morning, I woke up, and my subconscious had done the work for me: Everybody has dreams, everybody has ambitions and aspirations, and everybody wants to become the best version of themselves. However, many people stay in the complacency lobby, patiently waiting to be invited into their best life. That common enemy has a name: procrastination.

We all procrastinate at some point in our lives. We keep thinking about exercising rather than taking the first step. We keep thinking about jumping in the pool instead of taking a dip in the cold water.

We stare at the train we just missed because we didn't buy the ticket on time or arrived a minute late. We keep waiting, hoping someone else will let us in until we realize there is no invitation to live your life on your terms, no permission to be granted.

Don't wait for permission to live your best life.

Take the shot, even if you miss it.

My why is to help you find alignment between your values, identity, vision, and actions so that you achieve results and live your best life. Once you have that alignment, it's about getting your hands dirty and writing your own story the way you want it to be told.

Change starts with a why: championing a cause, setting a role model for your children, impacting your community . . . Without a strong why, it's difficult to start and even more difficult to maintain momentum, so understanding your why is your ground zero. A why is the engine of change and transformation, the Big Bang of your life.

Your why is your reason. The word 'motivation' comes from the Latin word *movere*, which means to move. It's the force that guides your actions and behaviours, unlocking your chain of reaction. True motivation is personal and intrinsic: it must come from within. The closer the connection between your desired outcome and your why, the stronger the motivation. If you want motivation in life, make that motive truly yours and internalize it. When you say you are not motivated, it's worth going a step back and assessing how strong and authentic your why is.

What is your why?

Here are some real stories of people who found their why and managed to successfully unlock their chain of reaction:

A New Beginning

My good friend Ana recently went through an unexpected and traumatic divorce. Her husband of ten years left overnight without any warning, and she became a divorcee mum of two young children in her mid-forties in a foreign country. She was initially devastated and thought her best days were behind her. The initial weeks were full of tears, resentment, and anger. She felt lost and heartbroken, and she cried until she had no tears left. In the following weeks, she slipped into a spiral of binge eating, TV, and poor sleep, leaving her depleted and sad.

One day, she woke up, and when she looked in the mirror, she didn't like what she saw: anger, frustration, and puffy eyes. She hated the person she was becoming and felt guilty for not being her best around her children. At that moment, she decided she had had enough and promised herself a fresh start. She didn't choose the cards she was handed by life, but she could choose how to play them.

She decided that she was going to be in control and become her best self, physically, mentally, and emotionally. The break-up marked a before and an after, and she decided that the 'after' was worth living, too, or at least giving it a good shot. After years of sedentary life, she started to exercise because she wanted to look and feel good, inside and outside, but her bigger why was a reinvention, a fresh start, a new chance at life. Every day, she pushed herself out of her comfort zone and dragged herself to go for a workout at the gym or a long walk on the beach.

Ana went back to her identity and what mattered to her. One of her biggest values is happiness. Her life's purpose is to be happy, live each day to the fullest, and spread that happiness to those around her. For her, exercising is a vehicle to get there. It gives her energy and motivation to do other things she loves, such as socializing, travelling, and spending quality time with her children. She also wants to give love another chance, and she knows that by loving her image and being confident in her skin, she will be more attractive and open the door to dating again. Connecting exercise to happiness and reinvention is what makes her show up in her spinning class and leave the sorrows at home.

One day, she told me she decided to celebrate the beginning of her new self by creating a special event in her iPhone calendar—15 August 2023: 'Ana 2.0'. That's her why, her intrinsic motivation to exercise and ditch the couch for the gym, leaving resistance behind: the new identity she's creating one day at a time, her engine for action. She's not trying to reach an arbitrary number on the scale; she's creating the 2.0 version of herself—a fit, healthy, and happy woman.

A Dream Come True

When my mum turned fifty, she decided she was going to pursue her life dream: open a restaurant. She had always been a stay-at-home mum as my dad's job required moving countries every four years, and therefore, she had focused on raising her children, my sister and me. Mum was naturally talented at everything that had to do with hosting, from doing beautiful decorations in the house to cooking wonderful meals and being a warm host that made strangers feel welcome at home. She saw it as part of her role as a mum and wife, but it was a gift and, above all, a passion. She enjoyed discovering new dishes and spices and adding exotic flavours to traditional recipes. She found fulfilment in entertaining and having people connect through food and drink. Every time we moved countries, she found opportunities to learn about cooking; she took lessons in Asian cuisine when we lived in the Netherlands, as there's a big Indonesian community in the country, and learned about Brazilian cuisine when we lived in Rio de Janeiro. Her passion fruit mousse is the best I have ever tried.

When Dad passed away, Mum was in her early forties, and she was living in the Canary Islands. During the first few years, she managed to find different part-time jobs and land casual work contracts, such as ground staff at the airport, shop assistant, and English language teacher, among others. When she turned fifty, she decided she was going to open her own restaurant.

Her friends thought she was naïve and delusional. She had never done any business management other than running the household admin and had no idea what opening a restaurant entailed, but she had a dream and 600 euros of savings to bet on it. Sometimes, that's all you need: the inspiration to have a dream and the courage to chase it.

She decided to learn everything she could about opening a restaurant and starting a small business. She enquired about the different types of public funding available to small hospitality entrepreneurs on her island, La Gomera. She secured a low-interest loan to fuel her project, and she took the first step.

Even though the initial phase was often overwhelming, and the obstacles kept piling up along the way, Mum never gave up. She knew exactly what her motivation was: turning her passion into a lifestyle and doing something meaningful that gave her purpose. On the opening day of Telemaco, she was both the waitress and the chef, the boss and the cleaner, the host and the receptionist. She did both morning and night shifts and she didn't have a day off in weeks. She worked relentlessly from dawn till dusk and all over again the following day. Because the loan was not enough to cover all the expenses and the equipment, she opened the restaurant without a professional dishwasher, but it didn't stop her. She hand-washed hundreds of plates and kitchen utensils daily without a single complaint, even though her fingers were swollen and her hands were dry. She woke up in the morning with a purpose and went to bed at night exhausted but fulfilled. Her rock-solid vision made everything else flow: her plan, her actions, and her new identity.

Six months after the opening, my sister Vicky and I saved money and gave her a professional dishwasher as a Christmas present. To this day, she says it's the best Christmas present she has ever received and one that reminds her of the hard effort it takes to chase your dream. Fifteen years after its opening in 2009, Telemaco is still running and is the most successful restaurant on the island, with stellar reviews online. She no longer does the dishes by hand, and she has a full staff under her payroll now, but her why hasn't changed, and if she had to go back fifteen years in time, she would do it all over again, one dish at a time.

I once asked her if she had ever thought of giving up when things became tough and the cash wasn't coming in. Without hesitation, she told me that she had never thought of not pursuing her vision. 'What else would I do?' she answered, laughing. She had full clarity on what she wanted to create, and her chain of reaction was in sync. She aimed to turn her passion for cooking and hosting into a lifestyle (her identity and her why), deliver an incredible and memorable food experience for her customers (her vision), and show up every day to cook, hire, clean, host, and whatever else was required (her actions). Chasing your dream doesn't have a price tag.

A Passion for Languages

In 2003, I moved to China to work as an intern for the Spanish government in Shanghai. It was my first job, and I was both thrilled and intimidated to discover the Red Giant. I didn't know anyone there and had no idea what to expect. What I knew for sure was that it was an opportunity and I wanted to make the most of it and learn the Chinese culture and language to explore a new and fascinating world.

Having lived in various countries since I was a child, from France to Brazil, Holland, and Italy, culture and inclusion have always been part of my core values. I always craved belonging, and I loved the personal satisfaction of being able to speak with the locals and immerse myself in their ways of living. After having learned five languages, it was time to tackle Mandarin.

Before the internship started, the government sent me and thirteen other interns to Taipei, Taiwan, to do a three-month intensive Chinese course. We spent four hours every day at a private centre called Taipei Language Institute, where local teachers taught us conversational Mandarin and the foundation of the language. The course was fast-paced, and by the end of the session, I was mentally drained and didn't know what language I was speaking any more.

It was overwhelming, yet while most of my peers went for a happy hour drink or a tour around the city after the lessons, I would find a local coffee shop to do the homework and study the new words. I would purposely go alone to avoid distractions and write the new vocabulary on a piece of paper again and again until the rebellious words had sunk in. The learning process was slow and frustrating; I often wanted to give up, but then I thought of being able to talk to local people, read the signs on the street, make new friends, understand the waiters and the taxi drivers, and perhaps one day, host a business conversation in Mandarin.

The hunger to learn, communicate, and be part of another culture were the whys that kept me going, even when I wanted to give up. During the first year, I decided not to install internet at home so that my only entertainment would be the local TV that exclusively broadcast Chinese shows.

I fell in love with the culture and ended up living in China for over three years. Thanks to a lot of effort and many nights watching shows I didn't understand, I eventually became fluent and was able to have business meetings in Chinese. Twenty years later, I'm teaching my daughters Mandarin at home, and I hope they will develop the same passion for cultures and languages.

Although these stories are very different in nature, they all share a common essence: Our why is always linked to becoming a better version of ourselves. The motivation is different and personal for everyone and starts with self-awareness. For some, it's about health; for others, it's self-confidence; for me, it was about creating a new lifestyle that unlocked my potential.

You can also have multiple whys that pile on top of each other to build a strong foundation. You might have many reasons why you want to exercise:

- Finish a marathon
- Go on more dates
- Look more attractive
- Have energy for your kids
- Live a longer, healthier life
- Feel confident in your skin
- Age well and prevent illnesses
- Have mental clarity to perform better

The stronger the reason(s) to support a new behaviour or reinforce an existing one, the more likely it is to happen, so try to grow and strengthen your list of whys and turn it into your tower of motivation.

Your why is not better or worse than anyone's, but it must be clear enough to keep you focused, solid enough to keep you grounded, and inspiring enough to keep you on track when (and not if) resistance creeps in. You must know where you really want to go in order to be headed in the right direction and have clarity on what you want your land to look like.

Reflection

Building your tower of whys is a powerful exercise, as it allows you to reflect on your intrinsic motivation and answer three key questions:

> 'Do you want it?'
> 'Why do you want it?'
> 'How much do you want it?'

Go back to your identity and build your tower of whys one brick at a time. If you want to make things happen, you must persuade your most important stakeholder: yourself.

Falling in Love with the Outcome

Many books tell you to fall in love with the process. This book encourages you to fall in love with the outcome, and by doing so, you will embrace the process. Fall for the person you want to become, the version 2.0 of yourself waiting on the other side of effort.

Many things that are rewarding and fulfilling are usually not pleasant or enjoyable; that's why most people avoid them, delay them, or don't do them at all. However, humans crave the feeling of personal success, accomplishment, and the endorphins of conquering a new peak. In the documentary *I Am Bolt*, the Jamaican sprinting legend Usain Bolt talks about the solitude, the darkness, and the demons he had to face as an athlete when he was pushing himself, training when no one was clapping, and enduring when the body hurt. But he kept going because he had a bigger why: the hunger to become the GOAT (greatest of all times) in the world of sprinting. His bigger why was to become a legend in the world of athletics.

The secret to consistency is to fall in love with the outcome, and by this, I don't mean the specific result but the person you want to be, the doer, the finisher, the writer, the entrepreneur, the identity hidden in the other side of hardship. I don't always enjoy pushing myself to go for a run when it's cold, dark, and wet outside, but I do love the feeling of removing the mental fog and feeling sharp, fresh, and light, and calling myself a runner. Running creates a better version of me: a more patient mum, a kinder partner and wife, a more strategic entrepreneur, and a more focused writer. That's what I'm in love with.

My run always starts with a problem and ends with a solution, so even if it's not the best run, I still push myself to hit the road because I prefer to be in the solution mindset space, the mental clarity zone, the land of anti-procrastination. I love the identity I'm shaping one step at a time, and that makes me appreciate the commitment it takes to create it. The outcome makes me value and respect the process and its hardship. I embrace the brush that helps me paint the canvas because without it, I can't create a better version of myself.

I often struggle to jump on a Chinese class on Zoom when I have a busy day of projects and writing or when I'm feeling lazy. However, I show up because I love being able to speak one of the hardest languages in the world and communicate independently with Chinese friends, business partners, and strangers. I'm not always motivated to learn new characters and memorize vocabulary, but I love becoming fluent in a language that fascinates me.

I don't always find inspiration to write, and staring at a blank page is frustrating when you delete the same paragraph for the fifth time. But I'm still typing away because I want to be an author who inspires thousands to unlock their potential. I love touching people through my work, whether it's an article, a keynote, or a coaching session, and because I love the outcome, I have learned to embrace the process that takes me there, the road less travelled, the sweat that rewards the effort.

You won't always enjoy the process, but if you truly love the outcome and the person you aspire to become, you embrace the journey and appreciate what it takes to achieve difficult things.

Welcome the hardship because it's necessary; worship the effort because it's what creates results.

What Drives You?

Your why is your North Star that guides your steps, but every individual has different ways of getting there. Just like when you are sailing, you have many routes to arrive at the same destination; you can take a different course, cruise when the wind is in your favour, or motor when you are going too slow. Some take it easy and break the journey into different stages.

When we think of getting things done, we all have different drivers. Unlike the why, it's not about the purpose but the vehicle: what inspires you to get to the destination, what triggers you to get off the couch. For some people, particularly type A personalities, competition and winning are often strong drivers. Professional athletes, senior executives, or top performers in any field usually fall under this category.

My Mexican friend Ray is a top-level amateur triathlete. When he was twenty-seven, he was at a team-building happy hour organized by his company in Hong Kong. He made a random bet with his boss and colleagues, and the loser would have to complete a triathlon. Ray, who at the time was rather unfit and could only swim breaststroke, accepted the challenge. He lost the bet, and the next morning, he signed up for the Hong Kong annual triathlon and went shopping for a second-hand bike. With much struggle, two months later, he crossed the finish line of the triathlon at Disneyland and the starting line of something much bigger: a new passion and lifestyle. Ray started training, took private swim lessons, and started to compete in every single triathlon in Hong Kong and Asia.

Race after race, he started to perform better and shave a few minutes off each of the three disciplines until he eventually started to make it to the podium. Year after year, he kept improving, becoming a little faster, a little fitter, and a little better until he won his first slot for the world's top event in triathlon, the Ironman World

Championship, held once a year in Kona, Hawaii. It's extremely hard
to qualify, as you only secure a slot if you rank top of your age group
in another Ironman race worldwide (except for the charity slots).
In the past fifteen years, Ray has qualified ten times for the Kona
Ironman, bringing home multiple top-five trophies. What drives Ray
is the thrill of becoming better and the hunger to win. For competitive
spirits like Ray, the biggest driver is the next challenge and the next
race. He thrives in environments where the performance of others
motivates and stimulates him to reach new heights, although his
ultimate competitor is himself.

Not everyone has a competitive and hungry spirit, though. Some
people dread that type of pressure, and instead of being inspired by
competition and races, it gives them anxiety and makes them shut
down in their shell.

What drives my mother-in-law, Dianne, to overcome her
procrastination instinct is the social element. Dianne loves being part
of a group and that's precisely why she joins communities where
she can find peer support and group accountability. Being part of a
book club where she's going to meet other women to discuss a book
is what motivates her to turn off Netflix and read at night; being a
member of a running group is what gives her the positive pressure
to set the alarm for 4.45 a.m. to go for a run and have a coffee with
the other runners afterwards; joining organized golf tours and trips
is what gives her the drive to plan the holidays. Dianne knows she's
twice as likely to do something when she's part of a tribe and so she
has found many different tribes across her different hobbies.

Some people are driven by a bucket list, the idea that you have
a checklist of things you want to accomplish before you die. Many
people want to achieve big milestones such as climbing Mount
Kilimanjaro, writing a book, doing the Camino in Spain, swimming
across The Channel, or running a marathon. These big life goals
often require months or years of preparation, and the final prize
is what drives them to train, prepare, get fit, and set themselves
up for success. The 'bucket list individuals' are often chasing the
next item on their list, and that keeps the momentum going. One

challenge leads to the next, and the adrenaline boost makes them crave new adventures. They keep ticking boxes, and by doing so, they nurture the motivation to climb the next peak, and they ride on the momentum wave the same way a surfer rides one wave after the other.

Others are simply driven by a daily sense of fulfilment. Personally, I love achieving things and get a high sense of accomplishment when I finish a task and lay a building block on top of the next. It's like a project-based mindset that loves to have a new objective and work hard to achieve it. I love writing and find purpose in it, but what drives me to write? It's my next book, my next article, my next newsletter. It doesn't have to be something major like publishing a novel; it can be a new article for my website or a new keynote, but I know that I'm at my best when I set projects that require a start, a process, and a finish, ideally with a tight deadline. The feeling of finishing something—even if it's a submission to a publisher that might get ghosted or a workshop proposal that might get rejected— gives me a sense of satisfaction, and therefore, I choose projects that align with my priorities and my big why. Crossing things off my to-do list gives me purpose, no matter if it's small things, like paying the bills, or big things, like getting this book ready for you.

Your why and your driver are the two sides of the same coin.

Summary

- Your chain of reaction comprises four elements: identity, vision, action, and results. They function cohesively as an ecosystem, and for the chain to work seamlessly, you must create internal alignment and remove resistance.
- The most important step is to clarify and define your identity: visualize who you aspire to be and define what success looks like for you. Once that piece is clear, you must believe it yourself first and use the power of affirmative language: You are what you believe, and you act according to your identity and your vision.

- Sometimes, resistance sabotages good intentions, creating a gap between vision and action. It's a natural part of the process, and you just have to pause and reflect to understand where that resistance is coming from so that you can dissipate it.

2

UNDERNEATH PROCRASTINATION

What Is Procrastination?

According to the *Cambridge Dictionary*, procrastination is the action of postponing or delaying something that must be done, often because we find it boring, uncomfortable, or unpleasant.

Procrastination happens despite the person knowing that it has a negative influence or consequences. Bedtime procrastination is a classic example with three distinct components: you have no specific reason for staying up late; you are fully aware there may be negative consequences; and it decreases your overall amount of sleep at night, impacting the quality of rest and the productivity of the next day. Yet, in spite of all the reasons to go to bed, there's always an excuse to stay up late.

Forty-two point six per cent of adults report procrastinating constantly, with 20.5 per cent reporting it as a daily issue. Meanwhile, a meagre 15.6 per cent report never procrastinating. While some say they aren't negatively impacted by regular procrastination, others suffer from chronic anxiety and other physical and mental health issues. Studies indicate that the average adult spends 218 minutes procrastinating daily.[1] That's over three and a half hours thrown into the seducing arms of procrastination every single day.

---

[1] Jack Flynn, '20 Telling Procrastination Statistics [2023]: The Prevalence of Procrastination', Zippia, 4 December 2023, https://www.zippia.com/advice/procrastination-statistics/.

The most effective way to defeat procrastination starts with understanding its origin. Isolate the root cause so that you can address it first and then correct the symptoms. The four most common reported reasons for procrastination, in order of importance, are lack of motivation (41 per cent), lack of time (25 per cent), lack of urgency (24 per cent), and lack of understanding (10 per cent). While lack of motivation is the overwhelming number one reason, it usually teams up with other culprits such as lack of interest or passion, boredom, insecurities, lack of energy, frustration, or something else. Very often, the reasons overlap, and a lack of time coupled with a lack of urgency are the perfect combo to never get a task done. Similarly, a lack of understanding usually leads to a lack of motivation, perpetuating the cycle of procrastination, which never works alone.

In the workplace, the average worker spends an average of two hours and eleven minutes procrastinating every day. That's around 25 per cent of the working hours lost in the black hole. Most of it is masked under minor, trivial actions that create the illusion of busyness, such as reorganizing the desk, browsing aimlessly online, visiting the pantry for the fifth time, and doing non-essential tasks to avoid doing the essential tasks. That adds up to a total of twenty-three working days a year stolen by the procrastination thief.

If this sounds familiar and you struggle to complete your list of tasks on a daily basis, from simple things like sending an email or booking a dinner to important assignments like rehearsing for a presentation or writing a critical report, you are not alone. It's called chronic procrastination, and around 20 per cent of people report suffering from it. The prevalence of chronic procrastination has been aggravated in the past thirty years, impacting nowadays four times as many people as it did in the 80s. Some attribute this trend to the rise of technology and its widespread accessibility: more distractions equals more temptation, especially when they are at your fingertips. The twenty-first century could very well be called the century of digital procrastination.

Because procrastination is not a medical diagnosis but a self-reported condition, it's difficult to measure its reach with accuracy and precision.

What are the assessment criteria?
What is the threshold to label procrastination as chronic?
Are you a serial offender?

While studies and stats rely mostly on self-reported information, other related data reflect the increase in procrastination in society. In 2014, cat videos garnered nearly 26 billion views on YouTube.[2] A 2015 survey of 7,000 people found that procrastination was a leading cause of this trend. It was reported that the positive feelings associated with watching cat videos often offset the negative ones that stemmed from not doing something perceived as unpleasant or tedious. As much as you might love cats, if you find yourself watching cat videos for hours every day, it's worth taking a look at your procrastination barometer—or adopting a cat.

The Science Behind Procrastination

Science explains procrastination as a fight between two parts of the brain when it faces an activity that triggers a negative emotional reaction, such as apprehension, anxiety, fear, or boredom. It's a battle between the limbic system (the unconscious zone where the pleasure centre is located) and the prefrontal cortex (a much more recently evolved part of the brain that acts as your conscious decision-maker and planner). When the 'unconscious brain' takes over, which is often, the result is delaying or avoiding the unpleasant task that could be completed or started today. Doing so offers relief from that negative feeling, albeit only temporarily.

---

[2] Sasha Petrova, 'Cat lovers rejoice: watching online videos lowers stress and makes you happy', 19 June 2015, https://www.unsw.edu.au/newsroom/news/2015/06/cat-lovers-rejoice--watching-online-videos-lowers-stress-and-mak#:~:text=Internet%20data%20shows%20two%20million,social%20media%2C%20garnering%20mass%20followings.

Although it won't fix the issue, biology has a solid scientific explanation to back up why procrastination exists and is such a common trait of human nature. The limbic system, which is one of the most dominant parts of the brain, is on autopilot and operates by default. It warns you to stay away from anything perceived as unpleasant or uncomfortable and is designed to help you navigate through life using your basic survival instincts. It leads you to emotional and physical well-being by avoiding pain and discomfort. It helps you avoid not only physical pain but also anything that triggers a negative reaction in your body or your mind. If it's freezing outside, your brain perceives it as a threat and tells you to stay inside, warm and safe. Similarly, if you dread doing the dishes after dinner, your brain processes it as a negative emotion, and your limbic system tells you to stay away from the unpleasant task and relax on the couch, which is perceived as a pleasant alternative that gives you comfort and relief. The limbic system operates by default; it's your unconscious automatically responding to external situations and making choices guided by your natural instinct. Humans are creatures of procrastination by design; we unconsciously favour the more pleasant choice—the couch over the gym, pleasure over discomfort, and easy over hard. We are naturally wired for procrastination. But it's not all bad news.

The cortex, on the other hand, located right behind the forehead, is a weaker and also one of the last parts of the brain to develop.[3] It allows you to process information and make decisions consciously using reason and logic. It's the part of the brain that makes the critical difference between humans and animals, who are purely driven by stimulus and instinct. Unlike the limbic system, there's nothing instinctive or automatic about the way this part of the brain operates, and you have to deliberately trigger it in order to engage it. When it's

---

[3] 'The Teen Brain: 7 Things to Know', National Institute of Mental Health, https://www.nimh.nih.gov/health/publications/the-teen-brain-7-things-to-know.

not activated, the limbic system takes over again, leading you to do the most comfortable alternative: procrastination.

Action versus procrastination is the daily struggle of human nature: the conscious versus the unconscious, logic versus instinct. The only way to beat procrastination is to take the battle into the reasoning arena and rationalize your choices to make the right ones.

Passive and Active Procrastination

Procrastination manifests itself in many different and surprising ways. While watching cat videos for twenty minutes to delay writing a report that is due the next day is a classic example, there are other types that are much more subtle. It's the difference between active and passive procrastination.

Passive procrastination

It consists of replacing a high-value task with a low- to zero-value task. Instead of starting your work day and tackling the tasks, you keep digging deeper and deeper into the social media hole. Instead of waking up when the alarm goes off, you keep pressing the snooze button to enjoy five extra minutes in bed. Instead of writing the report, you draw circles and hearts around your to-do list. Passive procrastination is clear and obvious because there is no value added.

Active procrastination

On the other hand, active procrastination is a more sophisticated and elegant manifestation of the same phenomenon. Instead of doing something that is generally considered lazy and unproductive, like turning on Netflix when you are supposed to be completing a tedious admin job, you find a new productive task to do. You feel less guilty because you are doing something that also adds value, but you are still avoiding the task you are supposed to achieve by keeping busy. You keep ticking the more enjoyable (or least unpleasant) items on your to-do list and adding new ones just to avoid eating the frog, the least appealing task, the one that triggers the resistance button every single time.

For me, the frog is finances and accounting. It's the item that reappears in every list and seldom gets ticked because I always add a new task such as writing a new article to justify not doing the thing I resist the most.

Active procrastination is a strategic way to trick your brain because you overuse action to mask procrastination and keep adding new items to keep you busy, avoiding the one you must really tackle: your frog. Don't fall for that trap: busyness doesn't kill procrastination; in fact, it's often a distraction that derails you from completing the main job.

Reflection

Look at your regular workday and identify the ways in which you procrastinate actively or passively. For example:

'I always watch the news before I start doing my work.'
'On average, I check my phone every ten minutes without a particular reason.'
'Before starting an unpleasant task, I visit the kitchen or pantry by default.'

As you revisit your list, you will notice how some behaviours are isolated while others are recurring; some are clear manifestations of procrastination, while others are less obvious.

Reflect on how you approach your to-do list, particularly the tasks you are more apprehensive about, to understand your patterns.

Do you eat the frog first thing in the morning, or do you leave it at the bottom of the list, intentionally keeping yourself busy with new things?

Do you keep adding items to your list to avoid tackling the most unpleasant task?

Procrastination and Mindfulness

Most people are aware that they are procrastinating: You are either doing or you aren't; you are taking action or you aren't; you are on the field or on the couch. However, only a few have the self-awareness and curiosity to ask where the resistance behind procrastination is really coming from. Is it boredom, fear, insecurities, lack of purpose, or confidence?

Procrastination is only the tip of the iceberg, the manifestation of something much deeper that creates hostility from underneath; it's a symptom. It's not a reflection of the action or the task at hand; the task is just a task. Procrastination is a translation of your emotional state of mind and how you subjectively and negatively perceive the job that must be completed. Understanding the root cause doesn't solve the problem, but it brings awareness, which is always the first step to solving a problem: understanding what the problem is.

The human brain learns through a rewards-based process, a survival mechanism in which there is a trigger, an action, and a reward. For instance, the trigger is being cold, the action is finding shelter, and the reward is feeling warm and cosy. You can extrapolate this process to deconstruct and unwrap the phenomenon of procrastination. For example, the trigger is the anxiety resulting from a presentation you must prepare; the action is putting your laptop away and relaxing on the couch; the reward is the momentary relief of avoiding something unpleasant. As we saw above, you can blame the unconscious part of your brain, which always picks the most pleasant option: the (temporary) reward.

The most effective way to overcome procrastination is through mindfulness, using self-awareness, and leveraging the same rewards-based system to trick your brain into doing the tasks you want or must complete. By deliberately activating the conscious part of your brain, you quickly come to the conclusion that the relief that comes from not preparing the presentation is only temporary and an illusion. You also realize that the longer you put it off, the more guilt and anxiety you will feel. As you have less and less time, the anchor becomes heavier, and the temporary relief soon aggravates the negative feelings: stress, irritation, panic, guilt.

You can manipulate the system to your advantage and rewire your brain to focus on the positive results that completing the presentation will have. You will be less stressed, the momentary relief will become permanent, you will get the weight off your shoulders, and you will feel proud for being in control and taking ownership. Be aware of those feelings; write them down if necessary so that next time you tackle an unpleasant task, you consciously focus on the positives and enjoy the benefits of getting things done early: the reward.

With mindfulness and focus, you can reprogram how your brain perceives and reacts to a trigger, turning it into something motivating and rewarding. Instead of seeing a run as something boring and hard, you can trick your mind into focusing on the benefits and associating it with positive emotions such as feeling energized, clear-headed, and fulfilled. You teach your brain to fall in love with the outcome, the reward.

Exercise

Put the trigger-action-reward system in motion to start something you have been postponing or avoiding.

For example, your goal could be to go to the gym more often but as you've been struggling to keep up with it, the thought of exercising triggers negative feelings (apprehension, self-consciousness, discomfort). Your action is staying on the couch and watching movies, and your reward is the temporary feeling of comfort and well-being.

Use the same example but reprogram the trigger-action-reward system: Your trigger is the anticipation of the positive feelings and endorphins that exercise releases, which influences your action of going to the gym, which gives you your reward of feeling motivated and energized afterwards. It's up to you to decide what goes into the equation to turn it into a positive and rewarding outcome.

By using the rational part of your brain, you can deliberately convert the perceived discomfort or hardship into a reward.

Procrastination Is a Luxury

You procrastinate because you can.

That statement is uncomfortable because it gives you full ownership and responsibility. Procrastination thrives in the land of abundance and choice. Ironically, the more options you have, the harder it is to make a choice. Think of a restaurant that has a five-page menu versus the one that only serves the menu of the day.

Our ancestors didn't have a choice. They had to hunt, or else their families would starve; they had to find shelter, or else they would be at the mercy of nature and predators. A cancer patient doesn't have a choice. They attend their chemotherapy session on time, or else they might not make it to the next. A student might procrastinate for months until the exams arrive. Once the exam is around the corner, they start studying, or else they fail.

Procrastination is the by-product of a society that spoils us with a multiple-choice lifestyle. We can afford to delay or avoid the things that are unpleasant until we are in pain. We can afford to miss the appointment that is not a must until it becomes critical. We can afford not to do something until we are forced to do it because we run out of time and the grace period is over. My dentist always reminds me of that—that is, whenever I see her every two years.

On the flip side, the fewer choices you have, the less room there is for procrastination. When my dad was sick, he delayed going to the doctor, not for weeks or months, but for years. On the outside, it was procrastination, but that was just the tip of the iceberg. On the inside, it was a toxic emotional cocktail with other explosive ingredients: ego, denial, a sense of immortality, and perhaps fear of what the doctors might say. He stopped procrastinating the day he was so sick that he was left with only one option: seeing a doctor. He booked a flight from the Canary Islands to Madrid in October 2002, and that same day, he was immediately admitted to the emergency ward of the hospital and then to the intensive care unit. The moment he stopped having a choice, procrastination vanished. Three days later, he passed away. He thought he had a choice until he didn't. I lived the most dramatic impact of procrastination first-hand. That's perhaps one of the reasons that led me to write this book.

Procrastination will eventually lead you to action because you have no other choice:

You book the dentist because of the unbearable pain.
You fix the bill because you incur a penalty for late payment.
You run to the taxi because you missed the bus.
You pay a more expensive ticket because you missed the cheaper option.

Guilty as charged! I have been that person before. Procrastination is a luxury until there is no choice left. Eliminate the options, and procrastination will vanish.

The Real Cost of Procrastination

Most people see procrastination as a nuisance, a brake that prevents us from doing things sooner or sometimes doing them at all. Although procrastination is unanimously considered a negative trait, society has become lenient with it. We have learned to tolerate it and normalize it. We all procrastinate at some point, pay the toll, and move on. We arrive five minutes late, pay a penalty, miss a couple of opportunities, and life goes on. Procrastinating is not a crime; it's not stealing or lying, and it usually doesn't harm anyone, so it's morally acceptable, provided it doesn't impact the person next door. The consequences of procrastinating are, most of the time, bearable; otherwise, we wouldn't have the choice to procrastinate. As we just saw, it's a luxury.

We all know that procrastination is not good for us, but our tinted lenses don't allow us to see how bad it really is. A short delay here, five minutes extra in bed, a missed deadline . . . things eventually get done, in this case, later rather than sooner. How bad can it really be? What if you could quantify the real impact of procrastination throughout the course of your lifetime?

It's estimated that procrastination cost the US economy a whopping USD 70 billion in 2023.[4]

A 2019 research from Nationwide Building Society's PayDay SaveDay campaign revealed that procrastination costs people an average of £449 each year, or £29,200 over the span of their life in the UK.[5] This results from leaving gifts and holiday planning to the last minute and not putting money into a savings account.

As I was preparing the material for this book, I did a quick math exercise to quantify the impact procrastination has had on my life. I went back to different events throughout my life where procrastination had had a direct and quantifiable impact, and I wrote it down with the consequences. The exercise was an eye-opener. I have overspent hundreds of dollars by missing out on early bird deals for races and events I knew I was going to participate in. I delayed the entry, and by the time I wanted to sign up, the 30 per cent discount was over, or worse, I couldn't enter the event any more.

I once missed a work flight from Hong Kong to Hanoi, Vietnam, because I procrastinated on the journey to the airport. It was January, the weather was cold and miserable, and I took my time to shower, then I took my time to get out of the hot shower, then I took my time to have breakfast, and I also took my time to check Facebook before walking down the stairs. I was unconsciously avoiding the cold and the rain, convincing myself that two more minutes wouldn't make a difference. By the time I tried to hail a taxi, it didn't take the usual five minutes. There was more traffic than expected, and I waited for fifteen minutes, becoming more and more anxious until a red cab finally stopped. I arrived at the airport and sprinted to

---

[4] Madiha Hashmi, '30+ Procrastination Facts and Statistics You Were Not Aware Of', Quidlo Timesheets, 30 November 2022, https://www.quidlo.com/blog/procrastination-facts-and-statistics/.

[5] 'Putting things off costs people £29,200', Nationwide, 13 August 2019, https://www.nationwidemediacentre.co.uk/news/putting-things-off-costs-people-gbp-29-200.

the check-in counter, pulling my hand-carry trolley. As I reached the Vietnam Airlines desk, they had just closed the flight. I didn't make it. Of course, I blamed it on the traffic. Almost in tears, I started to look for other flights and connections. I spent the morning at the airport, rushing from counter to counter. I finally made it to Hanoi eight hours later, having spent USD 800 on a new ticket and feeling angry, frustrated, and embarrassed. When my colleagues asked me what had happened, I told them I had missed the flight because there were no taxis, but deep down, I knew the answer: I had unlocked the negative chain of reaction where the accumulation of minor moments had led to a procrastination tsunami. Two minutes do make a difference. I never missed a flight again.

I have gotten better throughout the years by both choice and default because becoming a mum meant that very often, I didn't have the luxury of delaying or not doing. Procrastination wasn't an option any more. If I delayed going to bed, I wouldn't be able to catch up on sleep in the morning; if I didn't fill the application form on time, I wouldn't be able to find a day care for my baby; if I missed renewing the passports, we wouldn't be able to travel and visit our families overseas. Procrastination was a luxury I no longer had, and time was an asset I could no longer waste. So, what is the real toll you pay as a result of procrastination? It's your time, your money, and your life. You are not stealing from anyone other than yourself. You are wasting your own precious minutes, missing the shots you didn't take, and sabotaging your own life.

Think of the different episodes throughout your life when procrastination had an impact of some sort, whether financial, physical, or otherwise. It generates frustration with your friends when you are late, relationship arguments that lead to the dreadful 'I told you so' discussions, potential health issues, financial penalties, tickets sold out, and missed opportunities you will never get back.

Of course, no one keeps an Excel table of every occurrence of procrastination to quantify its impact. Maybe there is a business opportunity to create an anti-procrastination app out there. However, if you stop for a minute and run the mental breakdown to measure the pervasive effect of procrastination, you are likely to reach the uncomfortable conclusion that it's preventing you from living a better life. It's not just a minor nuisance or five minutes lost here and there. Procrastination can cost you thousands of dollars and minutes every year, but we often don't see the real impact of small actions until we see the compound effect and the impact at scale.

Now it's time for the replay. Have a moment of truth to understand the real impact that delaying, not doing, or avoiding things is having in your life. It's only you and the procrastination mirror.

Reflection

Look at your typical day and week and make a ballpark estimation of how much procrastination is costing you.

How often do you take a taxi because you were too late to catch the public transport?

When was the last time you had a penalty or missed an opportunity for being late?

How often do you miss the early bird discounts for events, flights, or purchases?

What is the biggest price you ever had to pay due to procrastination?

Procrastination and Fear

One of the biggest drivers for change and action can ironically be fear: fear of not growing, fear of stagnating, fear of stalling and missing out. In life, you can never remain the same. You are either rising or you are sinking; you are either moving forward or you are drifting behind. The status quo is an illusion that goes against nature, physics, and time.

Imagine you are in a race, and you decide to stay still while everybody keeps running. Some are already ahead, others pass you running, and eventually, people walk past you because you are not moving. Life is not a race, but if you stay still, you fall behind. This thought is confrontational because it requires action, movement, and continuous change. The world is evolving, and the only constant is change. People around you are growing, new technology is emerging, opportunities are created, and competition is stronger every day. You are not alone in the equation, and the other variables are dynamic. You can decide to take the momentum and ride on the wave, or you can sink under the water and drop to the bottom.

When I think of the need for change, the first example that comes to mind in the business world is Blockbuster and its tragic end. Blockbuster was an American home movie and video game rental chain founded in 1985 in Texas. Throughout the late 80s and 90s, it dominated the American and overseas markets. At its height, the chain had 9,000 physical locations globally, with one store opening every seventeen hours.[6] The giant had become a household name in millions of families around the world and had earned the undisputed lead in the industry. Interestingly, the business model was founded on procrastination. Unlike what most people think, the main revenue didn't come from movie rentals but from late penalties. Instead of returning the movie tapes on time, usually after twenty-four or forty-eight hours, a large percentage of users took longer, and as a result, they paid a (procrastination) penalty, which was much higher than the actual rental fee.

In 2010, the company filed for bankruptcy and went out of business. The main reason behind their failure was because they didn't see the need to change and adapt. While the market and consumer demand started to shift to online entertainment, they believed their footprint was deep enough to remain immune. They didn't evolve their business model, kept betting for the archaic concept of late penalties, and undermined competitors such as Netflix, which offered a much more flexible, competitive, and on-demand alternative. Ironically, you could argue that Netflix's phenomenal success is equally due to consumers' propensity for procrastination.

---

[6] 'Be kind, rewind: Blockbuster stores kept open in Alaska', CBS News, 23 April 2017, https://www.cbsnews.com/news/be-kind-rewind-blockbuster-stores-kept-open-in-alaska/.

The biggest mistake humans can make is to live under the illusion that we don't need to change. The Spanish phrase *renovarse o morir* (renew yourself or die) explains it quite visually and dramatically. Back to your land, if you don't do anything with it, it's not going to stay as it is today. If you don't water it, it will dry; if you don't look after the crop, it will die; if you don't keep on investing in it, it will lose its value. Have a moment of self-awareness: Are you moving forward, or are you falling behind?

As we saw in the previous chapters, having a strong why gives you the intrinsic motivation to set an intention. However, in order to turn that intention into action, you must remove the hurdles along the way. Most hurdles link back to the same root cause: fear. Fear is often what stands between idea and execution.

Fear can take many shapes and forms: fear of criticism, of coming last, of disappointing others, of falling short, of failing . . . In February 2023, I decided I was going to launch a newsletter on Substack. I started to explore the platform and work on the design and the settings in the back end. I gave it a name, The Lemon Tree Mindset (the same as my book), picked my fonts and colour patterns, organized the sections, uploaded content, and I was ready to send the first release and make it public. The motivation behind launching my newsletter was fully aligned with my identity as a writer. I had a strong why, solid as a rock. Yet, before pressing 'Publish', I sat on it for a few days.

I had reasons that were valid (in my head) to hold me back from publishing it. I didn't know much about newsletters; the design was not fancy; the pictures weren't professionally taken; I was in the early days of my writing . . . the excuses kept piling on top of each other, and The Lemon Tree Mindset stayed there hidden in the dark. Then, I had an uncomfortable reality-check moment. What I was avoiding was my own fear of failure, of not being good enough, of being criticized by friends and strangers. I had composed a dozen scenarios of failure in my mind, and that prevented me from launching my project, sabotaging my own efforts. I wanted my newsletter to be a perfect five, but in my mind, it was only a three at best, and that led me to delay the launch and make it public. In reality, it was neither a five nor a three. It was a zero because there was no newsletter. Nada.

I knew I had to overcome my worst enemy and evict the imposter living in my head rent-free. On 10 February 2023, I published the first issue of The Lemon Tree Mindset by pressing the 'courage' button. I read that email so many times I could recite it with my eyes closed, but once I clicked 'send', I felt liberated from my own fears. I lifted the heaviest anchor holding me back: me. It didn't matter that it only reached a handful of people, that I had to edit a few mistakes, or that it didn't get many likes. All that mattered was that by pressing that scary button, I had conquered my fear and taken one more step to bring me closer to my why and my identity as a writer. I was painting my canvas. By removing resistance, my chain of reaction was in motion once again, and I was thrilled and proud to have created something that was meaningful to me, regardless of the outcome. Launching it was a reward in itself. That first newsletter was the most important one I ever sent because by daring to publish it, I replaced fear with courage and intention with action.

What are your fears? Are you afraid of doing things in public? Most people are: speaking, writing, creating, singing . . . you name it. Because doing anything in public is scary and requires vulnerability. People will judge. People will criticize. People will find the fault. The best way to overcome fear is to understand it so that you can conquer it.

Fear is human

In nature, fear is a survival instinct. It warns us against dangers and threats to keep us safe. In society, fear allows us to assess situations and mitigate risks. Embrace fear as part of your nature, and learn to domesticate it. Tame the beast.

Fear is not real

Fear is an idea you have prefabricated in your head about a possible scenario that hasn't materialized. Fear is your fantasy, your illusion. In the same way that you create fear, you can deconstruct fear. It lives and dies inside you under your terms and conditions. You have the power to control it and revoke those terms.

But fear is not your enemy

As an introvert, speaking in public used to terrify me. I don't mean only the big meetings talking in front of a hundred people but also the team meetings with peers, the presentations in English to senior leadership, and the group debates where all my peers were so much more eloquent and persuasive than me. I would much rather listen quietly in my corner and digest information silently than get under the spotlight.

My fear of being judged in public was neither helpful nor beneficial. It prevented me from sharing my thoughts, building authority, and gaining exposure to new opportunities. As a non-native English speaker, I was more worried about how I sounded and my accent than what my message actually was. By the time I braced myself with the courage to speak up, either someone else had stolen my thunder, or the meeting had moved on to the next point and I had missed my opportunity. To make things worse, it was often the same colleagues speaking again and again, and their ideas were not even that interesting or groundbreaking. Their biggest advantage was that they dared to speak up. Either they didn't have the fear of speaking in public, or they had overcome it. How was I going to conquer my fear?

I decided to reinvent my relationship with fear and turn it to my advantage. When humans are scared, the resulting stress causes blood cortisol to rise. Cortisol is also known as the stress hormone and generally leads your mind and body to go into a defensive fight or flight mode: your body gets stiff, your hands start sweating, and your pulse quickens. Some people start trembling and have their pupils dilate. Others even blush, like my brilliant colleague Ivanka, who had a skin reaction every time she spoke in public, and her neck became a red patch. I don't have those extreme physical symptoms, but my throat dries up, my body becomes rigid, and I breathe and speak faster without realizing it.

These symptoms, usually perceived as impairing, don't have to be negative or debilitating. In fact, they are the exact same feelings athletes experience at the starting line of a race when the marshal is about to blow the whistle. The boost of adrenaline provides energy and focus to perform. It makes competitors alert. Inspired by my triathlon coach, I learned how to trick my mind by replacing 'I'm nervous' with 'I'm excited' and turn the darkness of fear into the light of excitement. Courage grows from fear.

Today, I speak in public in front of large audiences, both in person and virtually. I'm still intimidated by the large crowds staring at me, but instead of shying away from my fear or being in denial about it, I reframe it into a positive mindset of energy and anticipation. Look at how you approach fear and reinvent your relationship with it. Fear is not against you but with you, or rather, within you. Be aware of not only your fears but also how you react to them, physically and mentally. You can turn fear from your enemy to your ally.

Fear is the only fear

As Roosevelt once famously said, 'The only thing there is to fear is fear itself.' The human brain is very creative at ideating worst-case scenarios of all sorts. Before my first podcast appearance in The Trusted Authority Podcast in August 2022, I was terrified of making a fool out of myself. I had ideated five possible scenarios where things went wrong, from losing my train of thought to stating the obvious or sounding unprofessional. Then, I asked myself, 'What's the worst that can happen?' Even in the worst-case scenario of no one listening to the podcast, I would still gain something from the experience, and I did. I took the pressure off and spoke my heart and my mind, letting my fears aside.

Now, a couple of years later, I have spoken in over fifty podcasts and interviews. Some of them were spontaneous and had minimum preparation because practice gave me the confidence to show up without a script. I also started co-hosting LinkedIn Live sessions on a weekly basis, where the pressure was higher because they were live. In one of them, my co-host had technical issues and suddenly dropped off, leaving me alone on the virtual stage with over fifty participants in attendance. That was one of the worst-case scenarios I could possibly have envisioned: alone on camera without a plan B. I took a deep breath, made a joke about being left alone, and kept talking about the topic without panicking. The world didn't end.

In my first open-water swim race ever, the worst-case scenario became a reality: I finished last in my age group. The race took place in July 2010 in Big Wave Bay in Hong Kong, and ended at Sheko Beach. We were over 100 swimmers across different age groups. The race was 3 kilometres in the open water. The worst-case scenario was drowning, and the second was being last in the race. As I was about to finish the swim after well over an hour, I looked at the beach, and it was crowded. Most swimmers had already finished and had become spectators, cheering for their peers. I swam to the beach, and once I was out of the water, I sprinted the last few metres on the warm sand to cross the official finish line. I had come last in my age group, just a few minutes before the very last swimmer. In my head, that was a terror scenario of pure shame where I would be mortified.

Was it that bad? I didn't drown. I loved the experience and felt an incredible sense of achievement and fulfilment. I sprinted even though I knew I was coming last. That swim encouraged me to join a triathlon club, and I went on to complete over 100 races. The world didn't end, and I killed the fear of coming last. The worst-case scenario wasn't that bad after all!

Fear is only the beginning of courage

You can't have courage without fear. What scares you is an opportunity to be brave. Your fear today, your courage tomorrow.

Only you know your fears, and only you can overcome them. If you are afraid of speaking in public, good; grab the microphone and own the stage. If you are afraid your idea sounds silly, good; it's your opportunity to test your voice. If you are afraid of failing, good; use that fear to focus and do your best.

Know your fear and how it impacts you and change the narrative. Fear doesn't own you; you own your fear

Reflection

Think of a big goal you want to achieve but are facing resistance and hesitation. Reflect on how fear is holding you back.

For example, 'I want to start writing on social media, but I'm afraid of being judged and criticized. I'm scared of coming across as self-centred, and I'm intimidated by putting myself out there.'

Verbalize your fears so that you can understand them and then deconstruct them.

Six Types of Procrastinators

Procrastination is only the tip of the iceberg, but the resistance generated from underneath is much more complex and goes back to your personality, your default mindset, and your cognitive wiring. Most people procrastinate, at least at some point. However, the reasons why they do so vary, as we saw in previous chapters. Understanding the type of procrastination you tend to gravitate to and why it happens is the first step towards finding effective remedies to mitigate it or prevent it altogether.

Below are six profiles to help analyse and understand the different variations of procrastination. Keep in mind these are just prototypes, and people can't be boxed into dictionary definitions, but personas are useful for identifying patterns and similarities across behaviours.

1. The Perfectionist

Perfectionism is procrastination in a fancy outfit.

Perfectionism is one of our worst enemies because although society glorifies it as an enviable personality trait and an extension of excellence, it tends to act as a stopper more than it works as an enabler. For many job candidates, it's the perfect card to answer the much-dreaded question, 'What's your area of opportunity?' Most take a confident breath and casually reply, 'I'm a perfectionist, and I have to learn to favour progress over perfection.' It sounds better than saying that they delay starting the engine because they are afraid they are not good enough.

My tendency towards perfectionism was nurtured by the French educational system. I completed all my primary and secondary schooling in French institutions in the late 80s and 90s, first in a public school in the south of France and then in the French Lycée in Brazil. At the time, the approach to education was extremely rigid, and there was only room for academically brilliant students. The system would make you or break you. The bar of perfectionism was so high that being good wasn't enough. You were challenged and pushed to compete and be the best. As a seven-year-old, I remember being terrified of handing in my *cahier* (notebook) to the teacher for the weekly review. The assessment was not about the spelling or the homework; it was purely to see how neat each cahier was: Was the handwriting neat? Were the words evenly spread between each other? Was it perfect?

Our quest for perfectionism comes from different sources, such as strict parents, a rigorous educational system, personality traits, or perhaps a neurodivergence type such as OCD (Obsessive Compulsive Disorder) or autism, but they all converge in the same spot: the need to be perfect and the fear of falling short and dealing with the consequences—a red mark at school, punishment at home, personal disapproval, anxiety . . .

Perfectionism starts with positive intentions and high expectations but often leads straight into the procrastination loophole. We don't dare press the start button because our work doesn't live up to the imaginary and often unachievable standard we have created in our minds. The irony is that perfection doesn't exist; it's a subjective and invisible line someone draws arbitrarily. What is perfect for some isn't perfect for others, and I know that my work is never perfect for me. It will never be because I'm not looking for perfection any more; I'm looking for progress and growth.

My first article on Medium was mediocre. It had two views, and one was from my husband. I now look back at it and know why it didn't perform well: The formatting was terrible, there was no white space, my readers couldn't breathe, and it even had some typos I hadn't picked up. The old perfectionist-seeker in me would never have published it, but I got over myself and pressed the scary button. That led me to write more and better and to learn about formatting and editing. It was the first of over 500 articles, many of which received thousands of views and virtual claps. It reminded me of the swim race when I came last. What was the worst-case scenario? That no one would read my work or perhaps that readers could criticize it. Well, the worst-case scenario wasn't that bad. No one read my first, second, or third article, but people started reading my work eventually. My formatting improved, my titles became more attractive, my storytelling became more inspiring, and in February 2023, I published my first e-book. This is my fourth book, but it all started with one (imperfect) article. Cheers to the anti-perfectionist!

Perfectionism is a smart wolf disguised as a lamb. It makes you feel good about not doing things 'just yet' because you are brewing the perfect plan and crafting a flawless strategy. Instead of focusing on launching your website, you obsess over the font, the colours, and the logo. Instead of publishing your online course, you keep editing the videos and polishing the format. All of those details are important, but they are irrelevant if your website never goes live and your course is never launched. While you are busy chasing perfection, nothing happens; your land is drying, and you are falling behind. A promise of greatness is just words and thin air. Perfectionism is not a proxy for action. There is, or there is not. You create, or you don't.

If you suffer from the perfectionism procrastination syndrome, you can only overcome it with one thing: action. A remedy for the perfectionist procrastinator is to replace perfection with progress and lower the bar so that you can see your target (more on the low bar later). Instead of focusing on a perfect website that has all the fancy functionalities you dream of, you can start by building a simple blog as a foundation and then add layers of complexity on top, such as carousels and e-commerce. That's how I launched my first website, www.veronicallorcasmith.com, using Squarespace. Instead of waiting to have the perfect LinkedIn profile, start with a simple bio and use it as a public CV that is constantly evolving. Replace perfection (a specific goal) with improvement (an ongoing journey).

A mindset trick to overcome perfectionism is practising more self-compassion and giving yourself permission to be where you are. If you are a beginner, embrace that you are in the early stages and mistakes are a healthy part of the process. If you are learning a new skill, don't take yourself too seriously. Everyone was a beginner once, and the mistakes you are making are the same ones that experienced people probably made when they started. On one of my first triathlons, I ran into the transition area from the swim to the bike, and I started running with my helmet the wrong way around. The marshals whistled, and I continued running, unaware that I was the offender. When they finally stopped me, I adjusted the helmet, giggled, and jumped on the bike. After the race, all the rookies gathered for a well-deserved carb-loading feast, and everyone shared their stories of the silliest things they had done. We laughed, embraced our imperfections, and continued to race and hit the mileage on the road.

If perfectionism is slowing you down, it's time to ditch the perfect plan. You don't need all the details figured out. You don't need a comprehensive content calendar to start writing online. You just have to plant a seed. It doesn't have to be perfect.

2. The Dreamer

The dreamer procrastinator is on the other side of the spectrum. They are generally creative and have big dreams and aspirations, but they get lost in the skies and struggle to land the plane and turn the inspiration into a concrete action plan. Dreamers are usually great at generating ideas and creating new scenarios. They have a vivid imagination but dread sitting down to translate the big picture into a step-by-step manual and a roadmap. Their chain of reaction doesn't work because they get stuck in a vision they are unable to operationalize. Because dreamers love the freedom that comes with dreaming, they often jump into the next project and get excited about novelty, moving from one idea to the next without any execution. They are often victims of the shiny object syndrome and are easily distracted by new projects like an enthusiastic child browsing the aisles of a toy store.

In the entrepreneurial world, the dreamer procrastinator might have an ambitious goal, such as writing a book, launching a podcast, or starting a business. Many of the connections I talk to via Zoom share big plans for their business and their long-term impact. They have brilliant and inspiring ideas backed up by a compelling vision. However, when we do a pulse check six months later, many of those dreams continue to be books to be published, businesses to be launched, and ideas to be crystallized.

Amy is one of my private coaching clients. I help her build her personal brand as she's starting her journey as a wellness entrepreneur. During our first call, Amy explained her vision for the business she wants to launch. Her goal is to create a virtual community where she connects the best talent in wellness to individuals and corporations who are looking for trusted solutions and providers, such as nutrition coaches, health experts, physiotherapists, and more. Amy has a clear vision of where she sees her business, and she talked about developing a franchise model, expanding the concept to Asia and beyond, and becoming the top wellness digital community in the region.

Six weeks after our first session, we had a follow-up call. My first question was about accountability and execution. I asked her what she had done since our first coaching conversation to translate her vision into a business plan. She had a candid moment and confessed that she hadn't taken any action during that entire period. She had kept thinking about the future, strategizing and dreaming big. She could visualize what success looks like, but she still didn't have a business model on paper. She hadn't ironed out the pitch to partners and potential clients, she didn't have a value proposition backed up by a business plan, and she hadn't created a budget. Amy was a visionary who had the ability to zoom out and look forward, but she needed help translating her dream into a 30-60-90 business plan and executing it. Amy was not procrastinating because she was lazy or unmotivated. She simply didn't know how to operationalize an idea and turn it into a process-driven roadmap. Procrastination was simply a symptom, but the root cause was a lack of operational skills and know-how in execution.

A simple remedy for dreamers is to assess their goals with realistic lenses and deconstruct them by creating an action plan and a process. If your dream is to publish a book, you can break it into phases and milestones that you need to hit every week and month: It could be a goal of writing 10,000 words a week, having your first draft ready after four months, deciding on a launch date, and working backwards from there.

In Amy's case, the remedy was to stop dreaming 10,000 feet above the ground and take concrete steps to help her turn her vision into a business. After the coaching session, we agreed on the next steps. First, she had to work on her elevator pitch and define her business value proposition in one sentence to keep her grounded. Second, she had to prepare a sales deck with the business model to appeal to potential clients, partners, and investors. The homework was to verbalize her dream and articulate it through a compelling execution plan.

If you have multiple dreams and objectives, it's important to prioritize and classify them into different buckets using criteria such as urgency, level of difficulty, or investment required. This priority-setting exercise will help you prioritize your goals and actions and focus on the low-hanging fruit. In Amy's case, we broke down the project into different phases based on urgency, funds, and monetization. Instead of talking about franchising the business, we focused on phase 1: creating the digital platform (an app) that would allow her to connect customers and wellness providers and match the demand and the offer. Dreamers need to take the first step, no matter how small.

3. The Worrier

The worrier tends to see the glass half empty and finds buts and objections everywhere. This mindset is often a reflection of a lack of confidence and insecurities and is commonly observed in beginners.

They tend to worry more about failing than about trying, and they are afraid of amplified worst-case scenarios with dramatic outcomes that are unlikely to happen or whose consequences are much less harmful than they make them be. They also tend to generalize and use isolated negative experiences to support their own confirmation bias about why something will not work.

For example, someone worried about becoming active on social media because of the fear of negative criticism and cyberbullying might bring up cases of friends who were bullied online to justify their fears. Someone reluctant to do a presentation in public might refer to an isolated situation of a colleague who froze on stage to justify why it might happen to them. They distort or exaggerate reality and fabricate patterns that back up their insecurities and feed the procrastination monkey. Worriers tend to be individuals with high anxiety levels who are more self-conscious and need control to feel confident. They worry about what others might think, how they might be judged, and what could go wrong. As a result, they procrastinate because they create mental roadblocks that prevent them from taking action.

As the founder of a publication on Medium called *A Smiling World*, I encourage my friends and connections who are interested in writing to join my community and start publishing their work online. One of them is Kate, a lovely young woman I recently met through networking in Hong Kong. When I told her about my writing journey, she was inspired to start her own. She confessed that she had written dozens of articles and short stories over the years but had never had the courage to publish them or share them with anyone. When I asked her why, she said she was worried about having her writing and personal stories under public scrutiny. She was particularly concerned about the optics at work and how colleagues and strangers might judge her and her talent. As an introvert, Kate dreaded public exposure, and although she really wanted to take her passion for writing to the next level, she had mental roadblocks holding her back. After our coffee chat, I sent her the details of the publication and told her the door was open whenever she was ready.

Two days later, I received a draft of her first article. It was a well-written, positive, and uplifting story about overcoming fears and taking the first step. Kate decided to use a pseudonym for her writing so that her real identity wouldn't be exposed. Although she was still worried, she overcame procrastination by finding her own way to outsmart it. Later that day, she sent me a message saying that it had been liberating to press the publish button, and she felt like a rockstar. Ever since, she has been publishing articles regularly and growing her writer's wings.

A remedy for worriers is to rationalize their worries and decompose them. As you write down the reasons why something scares you, you might realize that many of them are unfounded or subjective. Another useful strategy is to write down not only the negative outcomes but also the potential positive scenarios and consequences the behaviour might lead to. It could be the development of a new skill, growth in confidence, exposure to new people, new business opportunities, and more. Once you compare both lists, you quickly realize that the positive scenarios usually outweigh the negative ones, and learning outweighs failing because even in failing, there's learning.

Lastly, another effective solution is to create gradual exposure to what you are afraid of. If you are worried about presenting in front of a big crowd, you can start by doing a small presentation in a safe environment with limited exposure. You could even record the presentation at home and share it with a colleague for feedback. If you want to speak on your first podcast but are afraid of going live, you can opt for a pre-recorded session where you have the option to edit or delete the parts you are not happy with before it goes live. You can find creative ways around your fears.

4. The Crisis-Maker

This type of procrastinator is always in crisis mode. They thrive with last-minute adrenaline and are stimulated by tight deadlines and crises. They believe they perform better under stress and urgent timelines. Many students fall under this category, waiting until the night prior to the exam to kick off a studying marathon fuelled by a caffeine overdose. They have an irrational love-and-hate relationship with deadlines and curfews: They dread them because they give them anxiety, but they need them to perform as they only operate under the threat of an imminent ultimatum. Although this technique can generate results in the short term, when overused, it tends to lead to stress, anxiety, irritability, and missed deadlines. No one can maintain high performance in the long term when in a constant state of crisis.

The remedy for this case of procrastination is having a schedule and a clear roadmap of actions and timelines to help prevent the crisis and break the project into milestones. If you are always late, you can start to set alarms to give you a time check before the event is due. For example, if you have to be out of the door by 9 a.m., you can work backwards and set different alarms as reminders. If you have to edit a long article or a manuscript, you can break the project into chapters with individual deadlines for each rather than tackling it as one big chunk.

Having a committed timeline for the first draft of the project instead of focusing only on the final completion date can help mitigate the crisis. That way, you fabricate new deadlines, breaking the project into mini-projects with their own schedules. Another strategy is to make commitments with other people to create group accountability. You can study in groups or ask a friend to check on you and your project on a regular basis.

5. The Over-Doer

The over-doer has the good intention of achieving a long list of things, but as a result, they overload their plate with projects and commitments that they can't deliver on. They might overcommit because they struggle to say no, or they simply underestimate the time and effort required by the tasks they undertake. A typical example is when someone who is already maxed out at work accepts an invitation to join a voluntary activity such as a charity event or an employee network. They usually say yes to the new task because they mean well and have a positive intent. However, when the time comes to organize employee activities, create Excel tables, and call vendors to compare quotes for events, they fail to pick up the phone and create the table because they realize they have overpromised and don't have the bandwidth to deliver. They realize that tasks that are seemingly easy and straightforward from the outside, such as consolidating RSVPs or catering for an event, can become a burden in practice when they have to chase people, update budgets, and satisfy a gazillion different food requirements. As a result, they often stress over the many tasks they have to complete and complain about not having enough time, triggering a spiral of frustration and guilt.

A powerful remedy here is to set boundaries and have a clear and honest assessment of your disposable time to manage expectations of what you can and can't commit to. Learning to say no upfront is a critical skill, especially in the digital world where people constantly pull you into Zoom calls, coffee chats, and brainstorming sessions. Before saying yes to a new project, take a moment to pause and understand how much time and resources it will require from your side and whether you can realistically support it or not. Learning what you say no to protects what you say yes to, yet many people struggle to say no to volunteering requests, especially when there is a certain pressure behind them. It's wiser to under-promise and over-deliver and set clear expectations from the beginning to avoid disappointment.

6. The Rebel

The rebel procrastinates out of rebellion and defiance. This behaviour often happens when we question the validity or purpose of the task we must perform. For example, your boss might give you an assignment that you believe doesn't add any value to the business, or you are overqualified to do it, and it bothers you. You see it as a waste of time and resources. Another example is when you apply for a job interview, and even though you have already submitted your CV, the organization requires you to fill out the application form again by typing in the exact same information into their system, making you spend twenty minutes on something redundant.

The rebel questions the purpose of the task because they don't believe in it; there's no buy-in, and they see it as useless. They struggle to start and complete the action because they feel frustrated. This commonly happens in bureaucracy and administration and in the traditional corporate world, where things are often slow and inefficient, and you have to provide the same information twice because there is no effective internal communication.

A remedy for the rebel is to first seek to understand the why behind the task to be completed. This doesn't win the buy-in, but it helps to have a broader perspective and see the bigger picture. The problem is that often, even after understanding the why, they still don't endorse it. In that case, the best course of action is to acknowledge that the task must be done and is part of the process to achieve a bigger goal; it's a necessary evil. If you want to have a shot at getting that job, filling in the tedious form is part of the journey to get there. Take it or leave it, but accept that it's part of the process and move on in one direction or the other rather than wasting energy complaining.

When I was applying for my spouse visa to become a permanent resident in Australia in 2022, I fell under this category of procrastination: the rebel against the system. Even though my husband is Australian, and at that point, we had been married for five years and had two daughters who are also Australian citizens, I had to write extensive reports to justify that our relationship was authentic and genuine and support it with graphic evidence, such as Facebook pictures, joint invites to social events, and WhatsApp messages. I was furious to waste hours of my day proving that I was in a legitimate relationship with the person I had been living with for the past decade. Every morning, I procrastinated in front of the pile of documents and forms before preparing the next report. I lashed at the immigration system, vented out my frustration, and wasted brainpower fighting and resisting rather than doing.

One day, I decided I was going to stop complaining and focus on the prize: becoming a permanent resident. I couldn't influence the system I was going against, so I decided to replace frustration with productivity. The faster I was able to go through the process, the quicker I would be able to finalize it. That became my motivation: escaping the process I was rebelling agair.st and tackling the necessary evil. I submitted sixty-eight different forms and documents within thirty days, and my application was approved. It still took eleven months for my visa to be granted, but overcoming procrastination allowed me to obtain my reward: a visa that allows me to live and work in Australia.

These types of procrastinators are not mutually exclusive but rather profiles to help understand and categorize behaviours. Most people who procrastinate are usually a combination of them. For example, the dreamer who loves big ideas might also be an over-doer who puts too many things on their plate and struggles to take action. The perfectionist is likely to be a worrier who worries about negative feedback and criticism. You might also find that depending on the circumstances and the specific action, procrastination will manifest in different shapes. If you are a beginner at something, your fear of looking inexperienced might hold you back (worrier), whereas if you are very experienced and you are assigned a basic task, you might resist it out of defiance (rebel). Most of us wear many different procrastination masks throughout our lives, depending on the circumstances, but they are just that—masks that cover something deeper underneath.

Reflection

Observe the different profiles of procrastinators and select the ones that you tend to default to. Think of examples and patterns that support your choice.

Focus on a project or action you are currently struggling to get started with (e.g., exercising, writing, taking a course) and assess under what category of procrastination it falls.

The more you know about the resistance behind procrastination and what lies underneath the tip of the iceberg, the more you can mitigate it and overcome it.

Summary

- Procrastination has a scientific explanation: The unconscious part of the brain is wired to favour activities that produce pleasure and comfort, even if only temporarily. To overcome procrastination, you must actively engage the conscious area of the brain and overwrite your instincts. It's up to you to overrule your natural instinct and make the right choice.
- The compound effect of procrastination is alarming: You are missing out on opportunities, both tangible and intangible, and it's preventing you from unlocking your potential and ultimately living a better life.
- Procrastination is a widespread phenomenon that impacts most people either occasionally or chronically, actively or passively. What you see is only the tip of the iceberg and the manifestation of other root causes, ranging from perfectionism to fear and lack of motivation. You can only defeat procrastination if you know where it's really coming from.

3

REMEDIES

Meet the Anti-Procrastinators

As I interviewed dozens of anti-procrastinators to gather inputs for this book, I discovered they all have different strategies and tactics that help them minimize resistance and maximize results. Some are fans of strict routines, while others have more flexibility; to-do lists were a popular item most respondents mentioned. Some need a clean desk and a quiet room to be productive, while others love working outdoors and changing environments to boost creativity. There wasn't a one-size-fits-all formula for productivity, but are there some commonalities?

After analysing the multiple responses and insights, I noticed three elements were present across the board and kept recurring again and again, like a common denominator of productivity and anti-procrastination: self-awareness, proactivity, and processes.

Self-Awareness

The anti-procrastinators I interviewed were highly self-aware. They knew exactly what worked for them, what didn't, and their weaknesses and blind spots. As if they were going through a procrastination X-ray, they were able to articulate what they needed to do to make things happen and what their enemies and distractions were. There was no hesitation, and they knew how to tackle the frog—and eat it. They also knew that they had to continuously audit themselves to see what was not working and make adjustments. There was always room to improve, and they were always on the lookout for blind spots.

Proactivity

This group of individuals was decisive and in control, thinking and behaving proactively. They were constantly thinking ahead, foreseeing and planning rather than reacting to external factors and circumstances. They had a plan B in case plan A didn't work; they packed an umbrella in the bag in case they got caught in the rain. In fact, they didn't talk about fighting procrastination as much as they talked about preventing it, being two steps ahead, and setting themselves up for success from the first hours of the day. They were not fighting fires; they were preventing them. One of them said, 'The best way to fight temptation is to avoid temptation.' Instead of becoming frustrated paddling against the current, they were aware of the tides and found ways to go with the current or pick the route with less resistance and the most favourable tide. They were not reactive. Instead, they strategically placed themselves ahead to have a head start and ride with the wave.

Flexible Processes

The anti-procrastinators all had processes, both formal and informal, and there was structure and discipline in the way they approached tasks. Each individual had their own personal recipe developed through trial, error, and iteration. Most workdays looked similar, although not strictly identical, and were pre-planned rather than left to serendipity and inspiration. None of them highlighted motivation as a key driver, but they did emphasize having their own tools and rituals, such as morning and evening routines, calendars, to-do lists, and systems to plan, execute, and measure work. Productivity was calculated and premeditated rather than left to the mercy of goodwill and positive intention.

An interesting and surprising caveat was there was flexibility within the process. If they had to miss a workout because a work meeting had overrun, they would still go for a short run instead of calling it a 'cheat day'. If they were too tired to complete the report they intended to, they would still set a target of completing the first part. Although it seemed counterintuitive at first, the anti-procrastinators were flexible and adaptable. Instead of going for an all-or-nothing approach, they focused on keeping the momentum and taking small steps to see marginal improvement every day. In their case, it wasn't progress over perfection but rather progress over procrastination.

Scientific research was right. The people who were successful at overcoming procrastination were those who were consistently activating the conscious part of their brain (cortex), making intentional decisions to overwrite the unconscious one (limbic system). They didn't wait for their instinct to kick in in order to counterbalance it and overwrite it. They strategically suppressed it before it manifested its first signs. Anti-procrastination was conscious, rational, and calculated. Through self-awareness, proactivity, and flexible processes, it was possible to defeat the monster even before it showed up. My social experiment brought the scientific theory to life.

One of the people I interviewed is Edith, a great friend whom I have always admired. Edith is the type of superwoman who makes being a superwoman look easy from the outside. She has a senior leadership role at a recruitment organization, and in her free time, she does interior design and house renovations as a hobby. She's also a hands-on mother to two young boys. Edith exercises most days, does delicious home cooking, and her hand-written holiday cards are always the first to arrive in our mailbox during Christmas, even though we live on opposite sides of the world. She's extremely detail-oriented and is always on time, usually five minutes early. She remembers birthdays and special occasions and always looks the part. When I thought about people in my circle who are role models for productivity, the first person who came to mind was my mother; the second was Edith.

To test her, I sent her a WhatsApp message on 6 March 2024 at 1.04 p.m. Hong Kong time, which was 6.04 a.m. in Switzerland, where she lives near Zurich. It was a regular workday, and as usual, she had to juggle work, admin, logistics, and family in a packed schedule. I asked her as a favour whether she could send me her personal tips for being productive in whichever format she preferred. I deliberately did not specify a timeline; it was part of the experiment. It was an open ask without a timeline. At 6.32 a.m. her time, she sent me the first of three voice messages with a detailed list of personal tips and processes to get things done. She could have replied later. She could have left it for the evening or simply forgotten about it, but she didn't. It took her less than thirty minutes to tackle the task and share her Wonder Woman secrets.

Edith describes herself as a morning person. She usually wakes up around 6 a.m., but instead of immediately switching into action mode, she enjoys what she calls her indulgence moment: a warm cup of coffee in bed overlooking the lake from the window and talking to her husband, Philip, about the day ahead and their plans. It's a ritual she honours every morning, no matter how busy she is. It helps her set the tone for the day and start it on a high with mindfulness, gratitude, and positivity. She likes to go to the office early and is often the first person from her team to arrive. It allows her to be ahead and plan the workday before it starts. She likes to have a sense of projects and deadlines and mentally prioritizes the list of tasks.

Edith talked about visualization and how important it is for her to see the goal she's trying to achieve, whether it's renovating a house, preparing for a holiday trip, or organizing a company event. It helps her make the objective real. She mentioned that she had recently purchased a set of curtains for a new house she was planning on renovating because she could envision her project coming to life and what the house would look like once it was finished and decorated. She hadn't even bought the property at that point, but she was manifesting her intention, and the curtains symbolized it. It was her way of saying, 'I'm going to make this happen, and this is what success looks like.'

She also highlighted the importance of working on a clean desk. By clean, she meant not only a tidy desk without clutter but an environment where she is able to concentrate without noise and distractions. Because she's a visual person, she needs a conducive space so that she can have mental clarity. 'Clear desk, clear mind.'

When talking about processes to ensure things happen, she divided them into things that motivate her and she's passionate about and things that don't. 'Doing what excites you comes naturally; things just flow,' she said. 'The challenge comes when we have to do things we dislike, and we all have them.' She described how the most efficient way for her to tackle those unpleasant tasks is to make them visual and unavoidable, turning them into the elephant (or frog) in the room. She adds red time blocks in her calendar dedicated to her least-loved tasks, such as banking or reporting. Instead of evading the frog, she schedules a date with it so that there is no hiding behind excuses or busyness. It's her and her frog.

Lastly, she added that although she's an early bird, she knows that the only time of the day when she can enjoy a silent home is in the evening after the kids go to bed. That is a precious time free from interruptions such as emails and notifications, and she uses it to complete tasks that require high focus and concentration. After becoming a mum, she learned to be flexible and adjust her routine around her life and circumstances rather than waiting for the perfect time. She seizes every window of opportunity and makes the most of it.

As I listened to Edith share her routine, the three traits described above resurfaced in her journaling: she was aware of herself and her preferences, proactive about her choices, always planning and getting a head start, and she had processes to set her up for success all while remaining flexible.

The Self-Awareness Test

Great athletes, top performers, successful solopreneurs, and award-winning actors all have one thing in common: self-awareness. They know their strengths and build on them, and they recognize their weaknesses and work on them or ask for external help to mitigate them. The result is constant self-improvement. The better you know yourself, the more tools and resources you have at your disposal to be productive and achieve your targets. If you know why you struggle to do the things you want to and are aware of your blind spots, you are better equipped to take control and implement effective measures to help you reach your goals.

How well do you know yourself? My guess is not as well as you think. When I joined Apple as a Business Manager in 2012 in Hong Kong, I realized I didn't know myself as well as I thought I did. As part of my onboarding journey, I had to do a self-assessment exercise. I was asked to pick sixty-nine competency cards from a thick pack, read each one and its detailed description, and sort them into three piles: skilled, unskilled, and neutral. It was part of the Korn Ferry Lominger assessment. Each card represented a skill, also called competencies, such as managing vision and purpose, conflict management, drive for results, compassion, motivation, and many others across different categories.

As I started to flick through the brown pack, I read each card carefully and placed it in the respective pile according to my subjective assessment. When I finished the exercise, the blocks of cards looked visibly uneven. Most cards ended up in the skilled or neutral pile, while only a few were part of the unskilled one. I was comfortable selecting my areas of strength: things like learning agility and motivating others were skills that had made me successful in my previous roles throughout my career. I was also comfortable rating myself as neutral on skills where I didn't excel or hadn't had a chance to prove myself, such as technical skills. Where I really struggled, and it turns out most people do, was identifying my areas of weakness, or in the Apple language, opportunities. I was unable to clearly point out the things that I was not good at. I couldn't see my blind spots, my lack of self-awareness, or perhaps it was my ego getting in the way.

Self-awareness is an underrated skill but a critical one for unlocking your potential and developing yourself. It starts with knowing yourself at the most basic level of nature (biological self-awareness) and understanding your preferred operating mechanism for dealing with situations, both positive and negative (cognitive and emotional self-awareness). We all have a default mindset conditioned by our personality, DNA, culture, and preferences.

Are you an introvert or an extrovert?
Are you a thinker or a doer?
Do you thrive in structure or in flexibility?
Are you analytical or intuitive?
Do you need external motivation, or are you self-driven?
Are you risk-prone or risk-averse?
Do you prefer strategy or tactics?

While the list is endless, and you can take multiple tests to obtain your personality profile, the key question at the core of self-awareness is, *What do you need to be at your best?* Most people don't pause to reflect on these questions and take the comfortable path of borrowing proven frameworks from successful productivity gurus, hoping it will work for them and deliver results. However, unless you are genetically wired the same way and have a personality twin, how will someone's life manual work for you?

Nothing epic was ever born within the confines of copy-pasted frameworks and borrowed guidebooks. Successful people found success because they kept experimenting until they discovered the recipe that worked for them, and they wrote their own manual, one page at a time. I recently saw a tweet from a social media icon explaining his morning routine. He said he spends twenty minutes in the sauna, eats four eggs for breakfast, and starts his day at 9 a.m. after having done some meditation, exercising, and journaling. If I followed his routine, I would probably be dead by now, likely depressed and definitely bankrupt. What I like about his routine, though, is that it's uniquely his, and it works for him based on his personality, preferences, and lifestyle.

When I asked my business collaborator and friend, Melanie Staunton, CEO of Communicate, about her insights and tips to fight procrastination, she talked about conducting a 'personal audit'. She said it's key to analyse your habits and understand where your time goes so that you are aware of how you spend it (or waste it) and, more importantly, how you want to spend it. For her, much of the traditional advice about productivity doesn't apply: She's not a morning person and never schedules her first meetings before 10 a.m., as that's when she starts to feel mentally focused and sharp. She likes to challenge conventional rules and test and experiment with new ways of working rather than adopting mass market advice. While for the high-demanding tasks, she prefers to be at home in her office, she often takes her laptop outdoors and finds it relaxing and inspiring to sit by the pool or a café while doing creative work. The change of scenery helps boost her creativity and reduce the stress and mental blockage that often come from being locked inside the same room for hours, looking at a screen.

Mel said she's a big fan of the old-school handwritten journal. 'If it's in my diary, it's going to happen,' she explained, pointing at her black leather diary. As a business owner, she juggles client meetings with workshop design and presentations, accounting, business development, and more. Having a clear process to meet deadlines is key. Her final tip is to separate work from private life so that she has time to reset and prevent work from taking over the rest of her life, leading to burnout.

Your best self is not a copy-paste of someone else; it's an elevated version of yourself. A routine might work wonders for some, but just like with a suit, if you want a perfect fit, you have to customize it and tailor it to fit your measurements.

Reflection

Analyse your current work routine and identify what you need to change in order to increase productivity. Use the filters of self-awareness, proactivity, and processes to guide you in designing your ideal routine.

Think about your land and what it needs to be green and fertile. It's not just about watering it but watering it smartly.

Being Comfortable with Ambiguity

When I did the card sorting at Apple, one of the competencies caught my attention: Dealing with ambiguity. I put it on the side of the pack and reflected on it. Was it a strength of mine? Was it a blind spot? I then placed it in the middle, neither a strength nor an opportunity. I had never stopped to ask myself how comfortable I was with ambiguity. Having lived in different countries and changed jobs and industries multiple times, I made the assumption I was pretty good at it, but was I really?

Apple put a strong emphasis on developing that competency, so I started to pay more attention to it. To be a good leader, among many other things, you had to be prepared to deal with the unknown. Even in senior leadership positions, we had to create business plans without knowing what products were going to be launched until the announcement day. Sometimes, we had to deal with customer fights in the store over the latest products or the queueing system.

Once, in the middle of the launch of an iPhone, the reservation system of one of the flagship stores in Hong Kong broke down, and I was asked to leave what I was doing and take my entire team from the Causeway Bay Apple Store with immediate effect to the Festival Walk store to act as improvised security guards and help supervise the queue of customers. The lines of fans and resellers zigzagged outside the shopping mall like a gigantic snake whose tail kept growing as more customers joined the frenzy. I ran up and down the queue with a walkie-talkie, making sure the customers were following the process. I was visually stressed by the chaos; I frowned and looked serious. It was a mess, and I was all over the place trying to give instructions to my team. Then, something happened. As I looked around, in the midst of chaos, I saw other managers stop to chat with the customers, high-five, and even take some selfies and smile. They were not running (like I was), they were not frowning (like I was), and they didn't look stressed (like I did). Instead, they looked composed and in control. While I looked like a manager, they looked like leaders who were graciously dealing with uncertainty and change and were letting things flow.

Suddenly, I had one of those aha moments where I realized that I clearly was not good at dealing with ambiguity. The moment things deviated from the original plan, I started to lose my cool and felt uncomfortable with the lack of control. It was a valuable life lesson that taught me that things might not go as planned, you might not have all the information, but you can always jump into the driver's seat and take charge of the situation. You can take a deep breath, and instead of reacting in freeze, flight, or fight mode, you can respond and stay calm.

That incident, running a marathon up and down the queue of customers, taught me that being comfortable with not knowing is key to growing and taking risks. Sometimes, the road takes an unexpected turn, and we find ourselves on a different path. Other times, we have to make decisions without knowing all the answers, and it's up to us to figure out where the piece fits in the puzzle. Learning to deal with ambiguity and the unknown helps us move forward. It pushes us to put our hand up, even if we believe we are only 70 per cent ready for the job.

When I wrote my first book, I had no idea how to publish it. I started reading about self-publishing, and the more information I had, the more overwhelmed I became. I read conflicting information about pricing: some advised to price it higher to create a high-value perception, others suggested listing it for free to raise awareness and reach a wider audience. The lack of knowledge generated ambiguity, which in turn led to analysis paralysis. I wanted to be in control of everything; I wanted to have all the answers; I was waiting to have a clear roadmap of what my book launch was going to be like, and I had none of that. Everything was a guess, and I was frowning, just like I was in that queue, going into reaction mode.

So, how did I remove the ambiguity to move forward? I didn't. Instead of waiting to have all the answers and dissipate the fog, I embraced the mystery and the gaps that come with doing something new. On the one hand, I minimized it by researching and increasing my knowledge about self-publishing. On the other, I embraced the fact that most things in life are a guess, a good guess at best. That's the reason statistics were created: to obtain the best-informed guess with the information available to predict a future that is unknown to all. I embraced the fact that I would never have all the answers, but the more I learned and tried, the more confidence and clarity I would have.

After weeks of researching pricing strategies online, I set the price of my e-book based on my findings and my intuition and moved on. I had no idea how to select the book categories on Amazon, so I picked three based on how similar books were classified and moved on. I had no clue what would make a good cover, so I designed one, taking inspiration from covers I liked, and moved on. Embracing ambiguity allowed me to take the first step, get my feet on the ground and my hands dirty, and move on. Once I was in the mud, the only option was to keep moving forward. Funnily enough, I then changed the price, picked different categories, and even had the book cover redesigned by a professional. But in order to get better, I had to take the first step. By doing, instead of overthinking, I was removing the fog and dissipating resistance. I had to be in the chaos in order to find harmony. I needed to be on the road in order to remove the obstacles along the way. You must embrace ambiguity in order to find clarity, and move on.

The Blind Spots

Self-awareness allows you to play smart and strategically because it gives you visibility into your blind spots. You know when to push hard, when to pause, and how to obtain the best results with the cards you have in hand. Instead of having a narrow tunnel vision, you zoom out and get a 360-degree panoramic view: Knowing yourself is your competitive advantage.

Your most productive hours in the day are non-negotiable. That's when you are at your best and are mentally energized to do the heavy lifting, the chores that require brain power and maximum cognitive effort, but also those that trigger the biggest resistance, the frogs.

If you are an early bird, maximize the early hours of the day to get your top priority work done while you are laser-focused and sharp. If you are a late-night owl, organize your workday around it and leave your prime hours for high-demanding jobs.

If you lose steam as the day goes by and feel more lethargic in the afternoon, it's unlikely you will have the mental and physical energy and motivation to tackle the tedious tasks then. Don't swim against the current, and leave those hours for jobs that require less effort and generate less resistance.

If you don't like planning, force yourself to create a process that will keep you accountable and make the deadlines visible. This could involve blocking time slots in your calendar or using project management apps like Trello to help you track progress.

If you are not good with processes, find a proxy. You can leverage technology to create reminders or establish simple systems for getting things done, such as having pre-created templates for your reports or presentations.

If you are not good at setting priorities, find ways to develop that skill. For example, if you are a visual person, you can use colour codes to indicate the urgency and importance of tasks or flag emails that require immediate action. Draw your frog and make it visible and colourful.

If you struggle with ambiguity, sit down and work on possible scenarios to reduce the anxiety that comes with the lack of certainty. Then, work on the different action plans for each one.

To get the best out of yourself, ride on your strengths and find ways to mitigate your opportunities so that they don't become anchors that hold you back. Procrastination is a smart beast that tries to sneak in through your blind spots and will attack your weakest leg during your weakest hours. The best way to fight procrastination is to outsmart it by being self-aware and preventing it from permeating through the cracks. Developing self-awareness will help you seal the cracks.

Exercise

Identify the blind spots that are keeping you from being productive.

Reflect on each of them and how they are impacting your ability to get things done.

Next to each of them, commit to one specific action to help you lift the anchors. For example:

'I'm not good at planning and organizing my time. As a result, I leave many things to the last minute and often run against the clock to meet deadlines. I'm going to start planning my week on Monday morning and dedicate thirty minutes to building my agenda.'

'I struggle with stress and often lose my calm when I'm under pressure. As a result, I get too anxious and delay doing the things that generate anxiety, leading to more stress. I'm going to start doing a breathing routine every time I feel the first signs and count until three to get started.'

Emotional Self-Regulation

We all have different mental and emotional zones. Some days we feel positive, creative, excited, and ready to conquer the world. Other days we feel lethargic, negative, and even depressed. Our mood swings are based on a variety of factors: stress, health, financial stability, hormonal changes, relationships, energy, sleep quality, and more. Knowing how we feel is key to being able to regulate ourselves emotionally and go back to the green zone, the space of growth and action, the land of anti-procrastination.

When I was living on the Gold Coast in Australia, my oldest, Alba, then five, joined the local public school, Broadbeach State School. Every morning, I rode her to school on an electric triple bike, where I had both girls in the back. It was an impressive vehicle, and I was soon known as 'Bike Mum' in the neighbourhood. The first time I dropped Alba at the main gate, a big poster on a wall caught my attention. It read, 'What colour zone are you in today?' The sign had three emojis, similar to the ones we use on social media: a green happy face, a red angry face, and an amber meh face. It was a traffic light of emotions.

Curious, I stayed longer to read further and learn about the colourful emojis and the zones. I liked the idea of correlating emojis to moods. It was visual and stimulating. The poster then explained the different colours: red meant upset, angry, exhausted, sad, and furious; amber meant withdrawn, distant, disengaged, tired, and lethargic; and green meant excited, energetic, happy, and engaged. The colour-coded system was not only a cute sign but also a system for emotional self-awareness and regulation. It was both an effective reality check and a smart call to action. Before entering the classroom, the children had to do a self-assessment and reflect on their colour zone and their feelings and moods. That moment of introspection allowed them to understand their inner world and be in touch with their emotions and moods. That simple system led them to answer a basic but fundamental question, 'How are you *really* feeling today?'

Unconsciously, I started doing the same reflection exercise every time I saw the sign during drop-off and pick-up times. After dropping Alba at the gate, I would ask myself questions such as, 'Do I feel positive today?' 'Am I excited?' 'Am I anxious?' The days I was in the green zone, I felt great about it. Bike Mum was ready to conquer the world! But the days I was in the amber or red zones, it instinctively triggered the next question, 'Why am I feeling like this?' and then the next, 'What do I need to go back into the green zone?' No one likes to think of themselves as a red emoji that gets impatient at every traffic light and starts the day mad at the world. No one likes the red zone. That's a toxic land where only bad herbs grow: complaints, negativity, insecurities, complacency, and procrastination.

I then started to do an experiment. In the afternoon, when I picked the girls from school, I would ask Alba, 'So, what emoji colour were you today?' And the most amazing thing happened. A five-year-old had more self-awareness than most adults I know. She would tell me not only what colour zone she was in but also why and what she did to go back to green. One day, she explained that she was in the red zone because her friend Erin didn't want to play with her during the break, and she felt sad and lonely. Another time, she was in the amber zone because she had forgotten to eat her snack, and therefore, she felt more tired than usual and didn't feel like participating in the group activities. I was blown away. Do we all need to go back to prep school to learn the basics of well-being, emotional self-awareness, and personal growth?

The green zone is the Eldorado of personal growth, a land of creativity, action, and productivity. However, you can only enter it if you first ask yourself some very simple questions: 'How do you feel today?' 'What colour is your emoji?' 'What do you need to be at your best?' Self-awareness and emotional regulation are the gateways to change.

A few months before publishing my memoir, I had a red-zone moment that lasted for days. I woke up one morning, and as I was having my coffee, I read an email on my laptop that triggered me. My professional editor, Ian, who was in charge of editing my manuscript, declined to review it one more time after I had pointed out several mistakes that had been picked up by the beta reading group in the pre-launch phase. There were multiple inconsistencies, formatting issues, and a couple of spelling errors that he hadn't picked up. Having paid him USD 1,000, I expected an acknowledgment email with a sincere apology and a timeline for the new revision. Instead, he replied with a casual email, justifying some errors as 'minor', challenging others, and declining to do a final edit of the manuscript because he was busy with other projects and considered that many points were arguable. Infuriated by his answer, I started to ruminate in my head possible scenarios that involved angry replies, initiating a lawsuit, and discrediting him in the writers' community. They all had one thing in common: they were negative, vindictive, full of anger, and intoxicating. During the following days, I spent hours writing to Ian, sending him screenshots of new errors throughout the manuscript, and asking him to fix his work. Saying that I was mad was an understatement. My energy was sucked into a vicious cycle of blame, anger, and reproach. I was so busy being angry that I didn't realize I had turned into the red emoji from Broadbeach State School.

One morning, when my husband saw me in our bedroom staring furiously at my phone, he looked at me and said, 'I don't know what happened to you, but there's a really dark energy around you, and you are spreading it to me and the kids.' As I was about to charge against him and unleash my negativity in his direction, I took a deep breath and thought about what he said and my aura. It reminded me of the emojis at school. I then looked in the full-body mirror and saw an angry, infuriated woman I did not want to be around. My own image horrified me, and I started laughing, thinking about how ridiculous the situation was and how I had become the red emoji without realizing it. Dave looked puzzled. 'You okay?' he asked cautiously, trying to tame the beast in me. Suddenly, my body relaxed, I let the pressure off, both physically and mentally, and I let the energy flow.

'Yes. I'm sorry,' I replied. 'I just realized I let the situation with the editor take over, and now it's impacting not only me but also those around me.'

What I had to do was focus on getting my book ready for launch and make sure the editing was done before the deadline agreed with my publisher. Instead, I was letting anger and negative emotions take over my mood, wasting energy and time on something that wasn't adding value to me, and that was creating resistance and sabotaging my identity. I needed to go back to green, but I was stuck in the red zone, preventing me from doing meaningful work that was aligned with my vision. I embodied the profile of the procrastinator rebel who was wasting time complaining about the task instead of completing it and moving forward.

For the following two weeks, every morning, I went through the same mental routine when I was about to start working on the editing. I would approach the job with apprehension, thinking about my unprofessional editor and his unprofessional editing. *I don't want to do it. It's not fair. I have been cheated.* Then, I would intentionally self-regulate my emotions and force myself into the green zone by focusing on what I wanted to achieve and why, publishing my book, and furthering my career as an author. I took a deep breath, and as I exhaled, I let the negativity go. I then took a deeper breath and let the good feelings—motivation, gratitude, excitement, and ownership—soak in. Through mindfulness and self-awareness, I recycled my own soul and my energy, removing the resistance that was obstructing my chain of reaction.

My memoir meant the world to me, and I was not going to let anything or anyone get in the way of making my dream come true. With focus, I learned to reframe the task of editing from something unpleasant and negative into something positive and rewarding. Every page of editing took me closer to the finish line, and I couldn't wait to see the story of my life become a book. Ownership, responsibility, fulfilment, and, more importantly, reconnection with my why were the vehicles that took me back to my green zone and helped me realign my life's domino. I had to activate my conscious brain and let it overwrite my instinct and quiet the inner voice that told me to quit and complain. I used the trigger-action-reward system to overcome procrastination and turned the action of editing from something tedious and boring into a navigation tool to help me reach my destination.

That's how I redirected myself from red into green and focused on what my land needed. Every morning, I replicated the same mental process. I self-regulated my emotional state, took deep breaths, did the reframing exercise, and intentionally reset my mindset. Eventually, through mental reprogramming, I lifted my anchors, and the transition from red to green became smoother and effortless. The negative feelings gave way to positive ones, and the editing job became a part of my chain of reaction rather than a brake holding me back. I started to embrace the process and value the hardship of the journey.

I could remove resistance because I knew where it was coming from, and I had learned to mitigate it. I did not particularly love reading my book again and again, but I removed negativity from the equation and approached it as a farmer who wants to cultivate a great land and remove all the bugs and bad plants so that the good ones can flourish. Every new chapter successfully edited became a motivational token, a little badge of pride and satisfaction that cemented my identity. Instead of complaining about a poor job, my energy was now fully focused on doing an excellent one. I spent hours editing and re-editing. I took full ownership and learned about the various standards of editing, which helped me become a better writer and have a stronger mastery of the English language. I became more knowledgeable about punctuation and building in dialogue. I developed an eye for precision and an appreciation for detail. I had gone from a full red zone to a productive green zone, where only good herbs were now growing. I was not only doing the job but also learning, honing the skill, and becoming a better farmer for my land. By falling in love with the outcome, I was falling in love with the process and had tamed the procrastination beast.

We all want to be in the green zone, and it's easier to stay there than to try to re-enter it once you fall into the danger zone. It's easier to continue exercising once you have an exercise routine. It's easier to continue writing once you have established a cadence. It's easier to keep going once you have momentum, but sometimes, we have to transition from red or amber to green, and that requires awareness and ownership: intentional change.

So, what do you need to get in the green zone?

What is the process to unlock emotional self-regulation?

Awareness. Perspective. Ownership. Disruption. Reset.

If you are sitting in the same spot looking at the same thing, you are inevitably going to see the same thing. If you want to see something new or find a different answer, you must change your perspective. Remember those viral digital pictures where 50 per cent of the people see one shape, and the other 50 per cent see a different one? If we try hard, we can all see both, but sometimes, in order to be able to see the second shape, we need to look at it from a different angle, perhaps try a different screen, or take a break and look at it with fresh eyes. When you really can't see the second shape, you can ask someone to point it at you and guide you to find it.

A powerful strategy I use when one of my daughters is upset is to get to the floor on my knees and talk to them at their height. By going down, I try to see the world from their eyes, but I also want them to see me at their level so that we are the same, equals. By changing my position, I create disruption and reset both my perspective and theirs so that we can look at each other with fresh eyes and have a reset moment.

Instead of becoming increasingly frustrated with an issue you have been trying to solve the entire morning, stop what you are doing and try taking a walk or going for a run. Pull the brake. Very often, the fresh air and the mental clarity that comes with physical activity will do the trick and help you find a new angle.

Going to the green zone is not about changing the initial situation but changing the way you look at it, your approach, perception, and mindset, turning it from negative to positive, and allowing you to self-regulate your emotions. I didn't change the outcome with my editor, and I lost USD 1,000, but I did change my mindset about the situation and, more importantly, how I handled it. It was a matter of perspective, looking at things from a different angle and pressing the reset button.

So, how do you transition from red to green? First, you acknowledge that you are in red, and you take ownership, jumping into the driver's seat. Then, you take a deep breath, and lastly, you change the environment or create disruption, even if it's just going for a short walk or taking a shower to wash off the negativity. Disruption creates change, and change opens new perspectives. They say life is 10 per cent what happens to you and 90 per cent how you react to it. So take control and make that 90 per cent count.

Reflection

Think of a situation that usually triggers you and sends you straight into the red zone. It can be a small thing your partner does that bothers you, receiving negative feedback or reviews, losing a deal you have been working on for a long time, editing a report for the fifth time, losing a file because you didn't save it.

Observe the behaviours you usually exhibit (frustration, anxiety, anger, etc.) and how they impact your mindset and your ability to address and control the situation.

Ideate one strategy that can help you transition into the green zone. For example, do a breathing routine, take a five-minute break before responding to a negative comment or an aggressive email, or write down a list of things you need to do to revert the situation.

For example, 'I become negative and lose my confidence when I receive a complaint, and as a result, I go into fight or freeze mode. I'm going to take a step back and think of how to respond instead of reacting and losing my temper.'

Physical Self-Regulation

Exercise: The 80-30 Rule

A golden rule for being productive and achieving results is to look after your physical health as much as your mental and emotional well-being. As basic as it sounds, millions of people neglect sleep, overdo caffeine, use alcohol as a proxy for relaxing, and overindulge in low-nutrition food and sugars to combat stress. A healthy diet, hydration, quality sleep, and regular physical activity are critical to keeping your engine in optimal shape and enabling you to reach your peak physical and mental performance.

Exercise is a key component of physical and mental health. It increases blood pressure and blood flow everywhere in the body. More blood means more oxygen, which makes our brain perform better, enhancing the cognitive skills to process information, think clearly, and make decisions efficiently. Exercise also helps enhance memory and decrease anxiety and depression. Additionally, because aerobic exercise boosts your cardiovascular system and improves lung health, it can also help to increase energy levels. As you move, your heart pumps more blood, delivering more oxygen to your working muscles.

According to the World Health Organization, adults should undertake 150 to 300 minutes of moderate-intensity, or 75 to 150 minutes of vigorous-intensity physical activity, or some equivalent combination of moderate-intensity and vigorous-intensity aerobic physical activity per week.[7] In practice, that translates into a thirty-minute moderate activity a day, five times a week. In other words, you have to exercise 80 per cent of the days and do a thirty-minute moderate physical activity The 80-30 rule.

Exercising is not about killing yourself at the gym for hours or becoming a cardio bunny but rather adopting an active and healthy lifestyle and making smart choices throughout the day. It's taking the stairs instead of the lift or the escalator, replacing the commute with a bike or a walk when the distance allows it, and avoiding long sedentary periods sitting on the couch or in front of the computer. The key to becoming physically active is to incorporate exercise into your lifestyle and have a flexible approach rather than a radical all-or-nothing mindset. Exercise is not only going to the gym; it can be walking your dog, doing a Zumba session at home, going for a hike, dancing while you listen to music at home, or riding a bike with your children. Everyone's circumstances are different, and it's important to be realistic about your life commitments and priorities.

When I became pregnant and gave birth to my first daughter in my mid-thirties, I went from being a hardcore triathlete who was training twelve hours a week to doing low-intensity hikes with my baby in the carrier. It was a long recovery, especially as I had an emergency C-section, and I had to reset my expectations and lower my fitness bar. But as soon as the doctor cleared me, I took the first steps and resumed an active lifestyle adjusted to my new circumstances and priorities. Once I had my second daughter, I often took both girls to the park and did a gentle workout on the floor while I watched them play tag and go down the slides. As a working mum, my disposable time decreased significantly, and I had to be creative and find ways to stay active throughout the day. I often took the double pram for long walks and participated in parkruns[8] on the

---

[7] *WHO Guidelines on Physical Activity and Sedentary Behaviour, At a Glance* (World Health Organization, 2020), https://iris.who.int/bitstream/hand le/10665/337001/9789240014886-eng.pdf.

[8] https://www.parkrun.com

weekend, pushing both girls while they complained that I was too slow. I did YouTube Pilates sessions at home and installed a TRX on the terrace to do short thirty-minute sessions while the kids slept. Whatever your personal and professional circumstances are, they are only excuses to stop you from doing things that are aligned with your identity.

I usually schedule my exercise in the morning, after the children leave for school. Unless I'm sick or travelling, I work out most days. In 2023, my exercise app, Strava, showed that I exercised 295 days. That's not every day, but 80 per cent. A common myth is that consistency means every day. Consistency means there is a regularity and a frequency built-in: for some people, it's every day; for others, it's three times a week. Don't obsess over the 100 per cent, and find your sweet spot. I prioritize exercise in the morning because it gives me clarity and energy for the day, and I have more energy and motivation than later in the afternoon. The chances of going for a run decrease as the day goes by, and instead of relying on motivation, I prefer to rely on habits. Don't commit to motivation, commit to yourself.

Whatever level you are starting off at is your baseline. Whether you are recovering from surgery, trying to lose weight, training for a race, or starting a new sport, take it as your starting line and try to build a cadence. A twenty-minute walk is better than nothing, and you don't need to kill yourself to feel the benefits of exercising and enjoy the reward.

The Beauty Sleep

In December 2023, I spoke on a podcast called *MultiPassionate Like a Boss*. As we started the recording, the host, Jennie O'Connor, asked me the question I wrote at the beginning of this book, 'What's your secret to getting so much stuff done?'

One of the reasons she invited me to her show was to discuss productivity because she had seen my growth as a new writer across different platforms in a short time, and she was curious to know more about my tips for 'prolific writing'. The first thing I mentioned in my answer left her puzzled. 'I prioritize my sleep,' I said without hesitation. Jennie giggled, and after a short pause, she added, 'Wow, I would never have expected that answer. I thought you slept very little to get more time in your day.'

Society has developed a widespread misconception about productivity, leading us to believe that we have to be constantly busy, chasing, and hustling. In reality, it's not about finding more time but protecting quality time and managing energy, and the best way to do both is through rest, focus, exercise, and sleep. Managing time is logistics; managing energy is well-being. People associate productivity with the number of hours they spend working in front of their computers, but how many of those hours are actually productive?

The World Health Organization recommends adults sleep seven to eight hours a night. Anything under that benchmark over a sustained period has negative consequences, both physically and mentally, for most individuals. Sleep deprivation also impacts memory and leads to early dementia and Alzheimer's. Sadly, many people cut on sleep as a default strategy to presumably do more: Students stay awake overnight to prepare for exams, executives double down on caffeine to survive the fourteen-hour workday marathons, and entrepreneurs sacrifice precious hours of sleep in exchange for one more call, one more pitch, one more email, or just a glass of wine at the end of a long, stressful day. Adding one extra hour to our active day sounds like a great idea in theory: that one hour might lead to more productivity and results, but the opposite tends to happen in practice when we sacrifice the quantity and quality of our sleep. We feel less sharp and focused, and exhaustion often turns into anxiety and mental blur. It's a negative cycle that can only be repaired with sleep.

While productivity literature glorifies early birds and the 5 a.m. routines, scientific research has proven that each individual has their own circadian rhythm, also called chronotype. That means each metabolism has a different body clock, and while some individuals are wired for early sleep and early rise, others function better in a delayed time bracket. Early birds and night owls are not only made-up expressions; they are an accurate reflection of our biology. Back in pre-civilization times, when humans lived in the wild, they had to protect themselves against external dangers such as wild animals and natural threats. The tribe members took turns being on guard during the night while the others slept, patrolling the area and warning the group in case of danger. As a result, humans started to develop different body clocks, aka circadian rhythms, to increase their chances of survival. Some would go to bed earlier and wake up hours before dawn, while others would delay their sleep cycle. That strategy allowed the group to work as a relay, increasing the hours of night coverage and hence mitigating the threats. It was a natural survival-driven evolution.

Thousands of years have passed, and unless we work in certain jobs, we don't have the need to patrol our house or be up all night, but we still carry our preferred sleep cycle in our DNA. Looking at my daughters, who follow an identical routine and go to bed at the same time, it's obvious that my older is a night owl while my younger is an early bird who is up and about before sunrise, just like her mummy.

Are you an early bird or a night owl? Knowing your nature and preferred sleep cycle is only the starting point; what you do about it is what matters most. To have the best quality of sleep, you must synchronize your sleep patterns with your circadian rhythm as much as possible and build consistency in your sleep-awake routine. Experts recommend going to bed and waking up around the same time within a thirty-minute window every day and night, including weekends, in alignment with your body clock. Humans crave routine, and this applies to our sleep too. Sleeping in some days to make up for poor sleep on previous nights is not usually the answer, as it disrupts your body clock. That's why some days you might still feel exhausted even after a ten-hour sleep. You think you are catching up on sleep, but you are getting your body clock out of sync, just like when you travel across different time zones.

According to the international bestseller *Why We Sleep* by Matthew Walker, around 40 per cent of the population are 'morning types', while approximately 30 per cent are 'evening types'. The remaining are hybrids of both. I am definitely an early bird, and more so after becoming a mum. My prime time is before sunrise, and I know that the early hours of the day are when I can best achieve the highest level of motivation, inspiration, clarity, and concentration. I decided to do a little tweak and go to bed thirty minutes earlier (around 9 p.m.) in order to wake up earlier and dedicate the first hours of the morning to my high-intensity work, the one that requires maximum concentration and minimum distraction: writing. The results were mind-blowing. I woke up fresh and focused and was able to write an entire article before the children woke up. I gained thirty minutes of time, which equalled sixty minutes in productivity, as I had no distractions, and my brain was in its prime time. Time magically doubled.

In my first year writing on Medium, I published over 300 articles. Some were as short as one- to two-minute reads, while others were six to seven minutes. Most of them were written between 5 a.m. and 6.30 a.m. while I was in Australia, parenting my two daughters by myself. I would often wake up before 5 a.m., as the sun in summer starts to rise at 4.30 a.m. on the Gold Coast, have a quiet moment on the terrace watching the sunrise with my warm cup of coffee, and start writing on my laptop, sitting on the couch until one of my daughters would wake up. Even though I would often write during other times of the day, the results were not the same. I would not be as focused and concentrated, and there would be endless distractions during the day, such as noises from the neighbours, phone calls, notifications, deliveries, and ad hoc tasks.

As a result, I decided to protect the early hours of the day purely for writing and content creation, whether it was a draft for a LinkedIn post, an article for Medium, or a chapter of a new book. I would leave the tasks that require less mental focus for later, such as doing research online, updating my website, completing admin tasks, or fine-tuning the SEO settings for my articles. I also noticed that the results of my work were significantly better after a good night's sleep. It's difficult to quantify how much better your work is after your beauty sleep, but the key difference is usually in the ability to focus and make decisions with clarity and confidence. When you have given your brain and your mind restorative time to sleep, rest, and recover, you wake up with focus and perspective and are able to approach things more positively and confidently. You are mentally equipped to tackle life and business problems in a much more composed and rational way, and you dissipate the mental fog.

Very often, you find your answers while you sleep, not magically but because your unconscious has done the work for you. Most of the titles of my books and articles were incubated at night and would make their impromptu appearance the next morning. While you sleep, your brain is processing new knowledge, connecting pieces of information, triggering your memory muscles, and finding the solutions to your problems.

Sleep is known for its positive impact on consolidating memories and augmenting the subsequent acquisition of new information.[9] Increasing your sleep quality gives your brain the energy to do more things and the cognitive superpower to do them better. If I had to give anyone one piece of advice on how to be more productive, I would recommend analysing your sleep data and patterns and seeing what can be improved. Poor sleep is often both the cause and the symptom: You don't sleep well because something in your life is not working, and you are unable to fix what's not working because you are not getting enough sleep to think clearly and effectively. The result is a spiral of anxiety and lack of productivity where things get done poorly and inefficiently with increasing levels of stress. In other words, a lack of sleep triggers the perfect conditions to stir a procrastination storm. So, how do you fix your sleep? Once again, it goes back to the fundamentals of awareness: understand the problem first so that you can solve it.

---

[9] Susanne Diekelmann, 'Sleep for cognitive enhancement', Front Syst Neurosci, 2 Apr 2014, 8: 46. doi: 10.3389/fnsys.2014.00046. https://www.ncbi.nlm.nih.gov/pmc/articles/PMC3980112/#:~:text=The%20stimulation%20of%20slow%20oscillations.

When I was going through a burnout in 2019, I suffered the consequences of sleep deprivation first-hand. As anxiety started to creep in due to work pressure, it directly impacted the quality of my sleep, and I started to sleep fewer hours with more interruption and less quality. I was often up before 4.30 a.m. after waking multiple times throughout the night, feeling too anxious to sleep and too tired to wake up and function. When I was awake, I couldn't wait to go to bed, and when I was finally in bed, I was too stressed to fall asleep. I was living on caffeine and the spikes of adrenaline generated by the last-minute work requests and ad hoc calls. The year 2019 will go down in my books as the most unproductive year of my life. I didn't do any of the things that stimulate me mentally other than work: I didn't study, I didn't write, and I didn't read a single book in over a year. I procrastinated not only on doing unpleasant things but even on things I love doing because I didn't have the energy to face them. I was physically and mentally exhausted. I knew I needed to sleep more, but I didn't know how.

Around that time, my husband Dave purchased a ring called Oura to help him track his sleep. As a commercial pilot with weekly flights across different continents and time zones, he's always been very focused and diligent in his sleep management, and he had heard great reviews about the sleep-tracking gadget. It was a thick ring with inner sensors that monitor the heart rate and body temperature throughout the day and night. The ring looked chunky and unfashionable, and I made fun of him. As the weeks went by, I started to observe his new routine: He would wake up in the morning, have a cup of coffee, and check his sleep report on his iPhone. The app would download, process, and analyse all the data from the previous night and display a thorough sleep report. It broke the night into light sleep, REM, and deep sleep. It would show him when his heart rate reached its lowest level during the night and the lateness, that is, how long it took him to actually fall asleep. All that data combined would lead to a sleep score and a readiness score on a scale of 100. The ring also showed him weekly and monthly trends where he could see improvement or changes in his patterns. Interestingly, the report also provided qualitative insights and lifestyle suggestions. A higher heart rate than usual might indicate that he had had dinner too close to bedtime and hadn't given his body enough time to digest. A slightly higher body temperature, together with a more elevated heart rate, might be a warning sign to take it easy and let the body rest to fight fatigue or a potential virus. It would also pick signals that indicated stress or would highlight that he hadn't moved enough during the day and had been passive for several hours. Just by looking at Dave's sleep data, I became more aware of my own patterns and blind spots and started to ask myself questions. Am I always going to bed at the same time? Should I have dinner a bit earlier to allow more time for digestion and better sleep? Was I watching too much screen at night?

When June came around and Dave asked me what I wanted for my birthday, I answered without hesitation, 'An Oura ring!' He teased me, saying that it was too ugly, and we ordered it online together. It's been five years since I have been wearing my ring every day, but more importantly, since I became aware of my sleep at a whole new level and gave it the importance it deserves. When people ask me about the ring, they often have the same objection, 'But it doesn't improve your sleep.' And they are right: it doesn't. Awareness alone never fixes anything; it's like receiving a fantastic piece of constructive feedback that you don't act on. However, awareness leads to understanding, and understanding opens the door to ownership, which triggers action. In order to solve a problem, first, you need to acknowledge that you have a problem; then, you need to understand the root cause of the problem, and finally, you need to act on it and find a solution. Self-awareness is only the starting point, your ground zero.

Tracking my sleep helped me understand that I was going to bed too late and that I needed more wind-down time and a more effective night routine. It made me realize that my third cup of coffee a day, usually after lunch, was making it harder to fall asleep in the evening. I also learned that even though I exercise every day, I was too sedentary when I was working at home, spending hours in front of my laptop without stretching my legs and moving around to let the blood circulate. I started to make little changes based on what I knew about myself and my sleep, and the impact was life-changing.

Through the sleep assessment, I also discovered the negative side effects alcohol was having on me. I had never been a big drinker and used to limit alcohol to occasions such as parties and dinners. As a social drinker, I never saw alcohol as a problem, especially as I was fit and exercised every day. However, starting with a new stressful job in 2019, I developed a new habit. I would often come back home stressed in the evening, and I would have one glass of white wine after dinner on the couch while watching a series on Netflix. It was usually one glass of Sauvignon Blanc, just enough to give me the placebo effect of relaxation and mental decompression. As soon as I started sipping it, I would feel that my me time had started, and I was able to disconnect temporarily from the craziness at work and the cognitive overload. It was rarely more than a glass, and I never considered it might have a negative impact on my overall health. *How bad could it be?* After analysing the sleep data and stats for weeks, I discovered that on the nights when I had a glass of wine, my heart rate was overall higher than usual. It also took longer to reach its lowest level throughout the night, which is an indicator of the quality of your sleep. The sooner you reach the lowest point, the better the quality of your sleep. Having a glass of wine had a direct impact on the quality of my nights, and as a result, I had less REM and deep sleep than on regular alcohol-free days. When I drank wine, my body reacted the same way as when I was about to get sick. It had to work harder to process the alcohol, and I paid the bill the next morning in the currency of well-being when I woke up feeling unrested, even though I had been in bed for eight hours.

With my new knowledge about sleep science and the recommendations from my ring, I made some minor changes in my routine and my habits that had a remarkable impact on my physical and mental health, my sleep, and, as a result, my ability to perform and fight procrastination. I started to eat dinner slightly earlier to have enough time to digest and avoid going to bed on a full stomach.

I removed the glass of wine from my list of daily habits, making it something exceptional, and I also built a consistent schedule. Instead of browsing aimlessly on social media, I started reading a few pages of a book in bed before turning the lights off. While things at work didn't improve, my sleep did, and I was able to handle problems with a clear mindset. Waking up in the morning with energy and clarity set the tone for the day and enabled me to achieve more things and sharpen my decision-making. By not checking my email inbox and social media before going to bed, I protected my nights, and I was ready to handle the ticking bombs the next day after my morning routine. Waking up fresh and rested helped trigger the conscious part of the brain and let it take over the unconscious one, the limbic system that would usually gravitate towards the comfort zone and the seducing *dolce far niente*. I felt proactive and in control.

Enhancing my quality of sleep allowed me to start doing things I had postponed for a long time because I didn't have the energy, such as resuming Chinese lessons or reading at night. That's what sleep and procrastination have in common. Bad quality of sleep over a sustained period of time will sooner or later turn into procrastination because if you struggle to tackle a task when you are feeling rested and energized, sleep deprivation will only aggravate the problem. As ironic as it sounds, sometimes the answer to procrastination is to sleep longer and better and wake up fresh and full of energy, ready to conquer the next peak.

I'm not affiliated with Oura, and you don't need to buy any fancy device to track your sleep. I personally like to use data to quantify productivity, observe trends, and contrast them with my subjective assessment to paint a more complete picture with both quantitative and qualitative insights. The key point is to be aware of your own habits, good and bad, and understand how they impact your sleep and, ultimately, your productivity. Some people find that exercising before bedtime helps them to calm down. For others, it's the opposite; exercise overstimulates them, and they struggle to sleep if they do any cardio activity in the evening. Instead, doing some meditation or journaling while sipping a warm infusion helps them relax and get ready for their beauty sleep. Little changes, such as replacing screens with a book when you are in bed or doing some mental relaxation instead of watching a movie, can be extremely beneficial. By becoming aware of your sleep and the factors that impact it, you can enhance its quality and create a new routine that works for you and helps you be more productive.

Unfortunately, most people are not aware of the importance of sleep and how it hinders their ability to be more productive. They only have a general idea of how many hours they spend in bed and how they feel when they wake up. It's worth dedicating some time to understanding how your habits impact your nights and how little changes can make a huge impact on your productivity, your well-being, and your life overall. Yes, you do need your beauty sleep.

Exercise

Write down your typical bedtime routine: what time you usually go to bed and wake up; how many hours you sleep on average; what you do before turning off the light (reading, watching TV, scrolling through social media . . .).

Identify areas of improvement, such as having dinner earlier to allow for digestion, avoiding alcohol before going to bed, diminishing your caffeine intake, or setting a more regular sleeping schedule.

Regulating Your Environment

Your environment has a critical impact on your behaviour, mindset, and well-being. For an introvert, a busy place with crowd and music is often stressful and draining. It consumes energy and is highly distracting and overwhelming. For extroverts, on the other hand, large gatherings are beacons of energy and creativity; that's where they thrive. We are all different, and we need different environments to be at our best.

Depending on the nature of the task, sometimes a hike in nature is the perfect environment for ideation, while other times, it's a quiet room. Perhaps, for the least consuming jobs, it can be a vibrant coffee shop where lots of other people are working remotely on their laptops, and you can breathe creativity in the air. Some people love to work with light background music. Others thrive in silence— no music, no noise, just the sound of disparate thoughts resonating in their head before crystalizing into a story.

Some places inspire us, while others distract us and might even put us off. Creating a conducive environment that works for you is key to productivity. The Apple campus in Cupertino, California, is the perfect example. The offices are as clean and pristine as the Apple Stores. There is no mess, no clutter, and everything is open and spacious. It's a sanctuary for ideation. People are not distracted by the surroundings, and the only decorations are posters on the wall of classic ads and Steve Jobs' iconic quotes. Those who want a different and more relaxed environment can go to the gardens outside to enjoy a fresh breeze.

Every individual has their own needs based on their personality and preferences. People with ADHD usually need a space with no distractions or noise so that they can focus and concentrate. Artists and creatives, on the other hand, often strive in chaos and noise. Some love music to stimulate their senses. Woody Allen has often stated that his best thinking comes in the shower.[10] Steve Jobs found the inspiration to create the Apple computer while reading a 1971 article from Esquire about phone hackers.[11] Many writers use commuting and public transport as a space for ideation and creativity. J.K. Rowling ideated the entire *Harry Potter and the Sorcerer's Stone* while stuck in a train for four hours.[12] Your best work is often incubated in the least expected places and not in front of a screen.

---

[10] 'Daily Rituals – Woody Allen', *Meaning Ring – Read Books. Get Ideas.*, 2015, https://meaningring.com/2015/04/25/daily-rituals-allen-by-mason-currey/.

[11] Charles Cooper, 'The 1971 article that inspired Steve Jobs', CBS News, 11 October 2011, https://www.cbsnews.com/news/the-1971-article-that-inspired-steve-jobs/.

[12] 'How J.K. Rowling Created Harry Potter', Newsweek, 16 October 2016, https://www.newsweek.com/how-jk-rowling-created-harry-potter-510042#: ~:text=It%20gave%20me%20the%20full,that%20delayed%20the%20 book's%20completion.

A conducive environment for productivity is traditionally associated with a clean desk and a quiet office, but is it really? What works for one individual might not work for another, even if the task to be completed is exactly the same. Additionally, different tasks often require different brain muscles to be activated. Therefore, while working from a silent office might be ideal for writing a report that requires concentration and attention to detail, a run outdoors might be the best channel to do some deep thinking and find solutions and new ideas. For creative work and brainstorming, some people might prefer to have some light music in the background. I personally find it extremely difficult to feel inspired while sitting at my desk, staring at the computer screen. I seek ideas outside in nature while I'm running, cycling, swimming, or walking my dog. Contradicting all productivity rules, I have written many articles in bed, enjoying the peace and quiet. This book was written on my couch, my bed, my desk, as well as at the public library and many coffee shops in Hong Kong. I let my instinct and the circumstances help me choose the perfect office for that moment.

Likewise, establishing an effective routine based on your preferences and personality sets you up for success. The first hours after you wake up set the tone for your day. The morning ritual looks different for everyone, but you must know what you need to be at your best. For some people, it starts with reading; others have a meditation or prayer session. There is no right or wrong, but you have to cultivate a routine that helps you transition into the right head space. My good routine starts with waking up around 5 a.m. without an alarm. I then have a black coffee and do a twenty-minute passive stretching on the mat with an application called Pliability. Passive stretching means that there are no active movements— everything is passive and slow with intentional breathing. Each pose lasts two to three minutes and allows the full body to stretch and the mind to relax. It ends with a couple of minutes lying on the floor with the eyes closed, just soaking in the benefits of the session and embracing the stillness of the moment. After a few deep breaths, I open my eyes, and I'm ready to start my workday on a positive note. I then open my laptop and usually get one solid hour of work in before my daughters wake up. One hour doesn't sound like much, but that hour is critical to setting me up for a successful day. I catch up on new emails, get a sense of the day, and identify the critical tasks ahead. If there are any major issues, I don't panic. I take a step back, zoom out, and try to see the big picture first. I don't start fighting fires. I'm in planning mode, in control, on top of my day. I don't react. I simply observe, pause, think, and respond. A morning routine is a cheat sheet for getting ahead and being intentional. By 6 a.m., I have full clarity on what I want to accomplish during the day and how I'm going to structure it and set priorities.

My bad routine is the exact opposite. I wake up later, possibly because I stayed up watching Netflix and went to bed late the previous night. I miss the stretching session, convincing myself that skipping one session doesn't really make a difference, and by the time I check the emails, any minor issues throw me off guard, and I start to derail. I then switch to reactive mode, jumping to fight fires. I dive straight into problem-solving mode and lose the focus and clarity that a good routine provides. The virtuous cycle quickly turns into a vicious one, where one bad decision triggers the next.

It's often difficult to identify bad behaviours if we don't stop to analyse our patterns because we internalize them over time, and they become normal. For years, I normalized behaviours such as jumping to social media first thing in the morning and checking my mailbox just to take a peek. I internalized having five coffees a day because I needed the spike in energy. Normalizing something doesn't make it acceptable; it simply indicates we have removed our filters, and operate on autopilot, silencing our inner critic. Unfortunately, where there's no self-critic, there's no self-awareness. The difference between a good morning routine and a bad one is day and night. It sets the tone for your day and defines the mindset that you will adopt to navigate through the obstacles that will get in your way. It's also your moment to strategize and prioritize. How your morning starts often preconditions the day you are going to have. Starting the day positive, calm, and in control allows you to preserve that same mindset throughout, in spite of the challenges.

On the other hand, starting your morning in a reactive mode is likely to carry through as the hours go by and possibly worsen as the tension escalates and unexpected issues arise. It's easy to slack and gravitate towards the bad routine. There's zero resistance, and it gives us the impression that we are saving time by jumping into solution and problem-solving mode. Those twenty minutes of meditation, exercise, or intention-setting are sacrificed in favour of action by rushing to the laptop and typing away. We feel productive because we are busy, perpetuating the fallacy that busy equals productive.

The value of a great morning routine can't be underestimated. It benefits not only you but also those around you, whether it's your partner, family, or team members. At Apple, the morning routine is also critical, and the leadership always protects it, regardless of the pressure, new product launches, or the amount of work ahead. Fifteen minutes before opening to the public, the leaders gather the teams in the store for the morning download behind closed doors. Besides going through operational updates and announcements, the most important part of the download is the moment of celebration and encouragement to empower the teams to provide the best experience to every single customer, living up to the company's vision: 'Enhancing people's lives.' The message is always positive and centred around the attitude and the mindset: focus on what you can control and set a clear intention for the day. By the time the doors open to the public and the first customers walk in, the teams look ready, feel ready, and are set up for success. I love the idea of being ready before you open the doors to your public: your family, your clients, your partners, and your team.

A fulfilling morning routine is the seed of a fulfilling and productive day. What you do the first one to two hours after you wake up has a significant impact on the rest of your day. It's important to constantly reassess your routine and make the necessary adjustments to get into the right head space.

Regulating Your Time

As part of my research for this book, I also interviewed and gathered insights from several self-proclaimed procrastinators, mostly friends, family members, and social media connections interested in the topic. Although they had different profiles, most reported one thing in common: a challenging relationship with time. Many said they struggle to keep track of time; others lamented that although they are always busy, they never get things done and are always running against the clock. They all shared a common frustration: a perpetual lack of time. Meanwhile, as described in previous chapters, the group of anti-procrastinators was highly aware of time and extremely focused on making the most of each hour of the day. The question was not how much (or little) time they had but how they could maximize it to make the hours last longer and count. They were successful at regulating and optimizing their time. It was all about maximizing time and energy to boost productivity.

In the personal growth space, productivity means how consistently and efficiently an individual can complete tasks and achieve goals. In other words, it's about doing more with less. The ultimate goal of productivity is to increase the quantity and quality of disposable hours so that they can be dedicated to things that matter to you and add value to your holistic well-being, your relationships, or your wealth. With mindfulness, self-awareness, and processes, you can increase your total disposable time, and the following pages will show you how.

The total disposable time is the remaining time after you have completed your essential day-to-day tasks. This includes things like your seven to eight hours of sleep, preparing and eating your food, showering, commuting to work, grocery shopping, and so on. This varies per day and per individual, but as a flexible, self-employed mum of two young children, I would put my total disposable time at around eight hours a day. If you are a full-time parent in charge of children and/or elderly, this might be less; if you are single, living with your parents, and working part-time, this could be more.

Regardless of your personal circumstances, there are different ways to increase your total disposable time.

Delegation

Delegation looks very different depending on your personal and professional circumstances. If you are a parent, you could delegate logistics to your partner or a grandparent. If you are a manager, you could let go of certain tasks that you traditionally kept to yourself so that you can focus on high-impact tasks. If you can afford to delegate some of the time-consuming tasks of your daily routine, you can significantly increase your disposable time.

Delegating requires priority-setting and strategic thinking. You must be able to prioritize the different tasks and assess which ones can be delegated and which ones should be performed by you based on criteria such as level of difficulty, impact, risk, and alignment with your vision.

An important part of delegating is letting go. Many parents, especially mums, including myself, struggle to delegate certain tasks to their partners because they want them done a certain way. Delegation comes with accepting that other people have different ways of doing things and being okay with it. I have come to terms with the fact that when my husband looks after the kids, they might not look as cute and colour-coded as I would like them to, but they always have a blast and come back with a huge smile while I gain a whole afternoon to work and be productive.

Automation

Automation allows us to free up time by leveraging technology to create systems and set certain tasks on autopilot. This can be as simple as doing grocery shopping online and having recurring lists of frequently purchased products to streamline the process. When I was living on the Gold Coast, I discovered how convenient online grocery shopping was and how much time it saved me at scale. After a couple of purchases online at the local supermarket Coles, the system automatically populated my frequently purchased items, and the entire shopping journey was finalized within five minutes, from the comfort of my couch. The alternative was to drive to the supermarket, park the car, and walk endlessly through the aisles, sometimes twice because I missed the item I was looking for. This is a basic example, but it's the reality of many households and proves the point that small changes at scale can give us time back. In this case, online shopping gave me an hour and a half of quality time back every single week. That's six hours a month and over sixty hours a year. The compound effect of automation starts to move the productivity needle.

Automation can be implemented in many aspects of your life, particularly with actions that have a recurring element in them, from paying for monthly activities to setting up autopay for expenses such as gym membership, school tuition, bills, and more. As a writer and content creator, I find that automation and processes are key in my workflows. I use features like pre-scheduling to organize my LinkedIn posts and my Substack newsletter early in the week so that I don't have to use more brainpower later and I can free more time in my day. It's one less task hovering above my head. It not only saves me time but also allows me to do tasks in bulk and increase productivity. I often pre-schedule two newsletters at a time so that I don't have to repeat the same task again. Likewise, when I invoice my clients, I have pre-created templates on the platform Invoice Simple, where I only have to update the details of that particular invoice, and the rest is automatically updated. It takes me less than two minutes to create a professional-looking invoice with my logo and brand colours already embedded in it.

Automation can also be a hybrid, whereby you use customizable templates or processes to make your life easier. In my work as a public speaker, I have standard files stored in my Canva Pro account for almost everything I can possibly need: flyers, keynote presentations, speaker profiles, and sales decks. Building a presentation on a pre-designed template that includes my corporate fonts, colour patterns, and frequent icons saves me at least one hour of formatting and design every time and a lot of frustration. When I need something new that I haven't created before, I always browse through Canva and find a template that can work as a basis.

If you pause and observe your shopping, working, and lifestyle habits, you will see many things around you that can be automated, such as autopay for bank bills, service renewals, software updates, and so on. Automating things ad hoc and only occasionally is usually more of a nuisance than a benefit, but when you start to see the ripple effect, you realize how powerful investing five minutes in creating processes is.

Outsourcing

In this context, outsourcing, as opposed to delegating, implies that money is paid in exchange for a service or a product. Many solopreneurs hire virtual assistants to help them with admin tasks and social media. They are usually flexible and inexpensive and can help with things such as preparing invoices and proposals, organizing event logistics, managing the pipeline of leads, and whatever else you might need remote assistance with.

When I launched my business in 2022, I realized that I was spending a long time in accounting and finances. As a one-person business, I was doing everything myself, and at the end of the day, I was spending more time doing the operational and admin stuff than actually planning and strategizing my business. I was not doing the things that I am passionate about. Instead, I was doing things that I am not passionate about, and I was doing them poorly. The urgent was keeping me from doing the important, and I was deviating from my purpose. It was a lose-lose situation. After a few months of frustration and inefficiency, I decided it was time to ask for help, and I contacted an accountant in Hong Kong who took over the financials and the monthly reporting. The arrangement worked: I was able to increase my disposable time and dedicate it to things that mattered to me and that I wanted to improve at. I came to terms with delegating or outsourcing certain jobs rather than procrastinating forever, letting them suck your energy and your soul.

What should you outsource or delegate? This is a personal question only you can answer, but try to outsource things that are not a priority in your personal and professional development, even if they might still be instrumental in your business. As a writer, I always outsource the cover of my books. If I were a fantastic designer with great digital skills or if I had a personal interest in that field, I would do it myself. I tried designing the cover for my first book, *The Lemon Tree Mindset*, and although it was a fun experience, the general verdict is that it looked amateur. More importantly, I decided that I would rather spend my time writing and promoting my book than designing covers. I then outsourced it to a graphic designer on Fiverr, and the feedback about the new cover was that it looked more attractive and professional. Since then, I have outsourced the cover of all my books and e-books. I learned what I had to say no to in order to become better at what I say yes to.

My approach is not to outsource things only because you can't do them or are not good at them. Everyone is coachable. Be strategic about what you want to outsource, ask yourself why you are doing it, and go back to your vision and your identity. As I was going to publish my first book, there was an option that was tempting as a new author: paying a marketing company to help with the process of self-publishing. They usually offer different packages that cover everything from the editing to the launch plan and the marketing campaign, listing your book on Amazon and Goodreads, pitching for editorial coverage, applying to literary awards, and more.

At the time, I had no idea about the publishing industry, but I was sure of one thing: I wanted to understand the process, even if it implied hours of learning and practice. I didn't want to delegate something that mattered to me without understanding it because that meant giving away full ownership. As an author, I wanted to own not only the writing but the entire life cycle of a book. I decided to learn everything an author should know and completed several courses and tutorials on Amazon and YouTube. My professional ambition is to turn my writing into a lifestyle, and that means that

I want to understand the ins and outs of that world before I pass on responsibilities to a third party, such as an agent or a publisher. That translated into spending hours online, researching topics that were totally alien to me, such as royalties and distribution. Once I felt confident, I turned my knowledge into action and self-published my first book. Shortly after, I also learned about paid ads and launched my first campaigns on Amazon and Facebook, putting the theory into practice.

It's important to outsource and delegate in a responsible manner because you can easily lose control over things that matter to you. Outsourcing can easily become a slippery slope as it's tempting to recur to it out of laziness or because it's too hard, especially if you have money to throw at the problem. Understanding what you want to outsource—and what you don't—and why will help you be intentional about what you let go. If you deeply care about something and it's closely linked to your identity, it's strategic to make an effort to understand the fundamentals before outsourcing it to a third party. Knowledge is a powerful tool to mitigate risks and have leverage.

Fighting procrastination is not always about doing but finding ways of getting things done and leveraging resources efficiently. The key is to identify what you want to delegate or outsource and, more importantly, why. Every time I delegated things that I cared about (such as the accounting reports or the book cover), I made sure I understood what I was letting go and had basic knowledge to drive accountability. Before I outsourced my accounting reports, I took multiple finance courses online and learned the fundamentals of a profit and loss statement and a balance sheet. Before I outsourced my book cover to designers, I did my research on how to design an attractive cover so that I could give the designer a detailed brief to set him up for success.

Asking for Help

An effective strategy to beat procrastination is knowing when we have a skill or knowledge gap (self-awareness) and learning how to ask for help (vulnerability). We all have our blind spots. We often think that we are better than we are, and we often think we are much worse than we are. It's difficult to do a fair and accurate self-assessment and see our weakest link when we are in front of the mirror.

When I finished writing my memoir in 2022, I was ready to take the world by storm. I started to do my research about publishing, consolidated the details of the main publishers, and started to send manuscript submissions left, right, and centre. The standard process is to send a couple of chapters together with information such as the book synopsis, the target audience, an author bio, and previously published work. I thought I had nailed it. I turned on the project-oriented mode and started to punch out emails like a pro. I reached over twenty publishers via email with the hope that at least one would show interest. Crickets. I didn't hear from a single one back. Not after a week, not after a month.

The only ones that showed interest were a special type of publishers known as 'vanity publishers'. I had no idea what they were until I read about them online and found out that they are companies that help novice authors publish their books and deal with the marketing and the launch plan. They sent me an email praising my book, saying it had a lot of potential, and after they feathered my ego, came the catch: a special publishing deal of USD 10,000 to help me with the end-to-end of the book launch. I was devastated after having had my hopes high that a publisher might be interested in my work. Most of these companies only want to grab money from desperate writers who would do anything to have their work published, and I was their perfect target. No wonder they are called 'vanity publishers', or the less complimentary term, predatory publishers.

That experience was a life lesson. First, it was an ego recalibration exercise: my writing was not as good as I thought it was, and in order to get the attention of (legitimate) publishers, I would have to step up my game. Second, it also made me realize that I didn't want to outsource something that I truly cared about (my writing and my book) without understanding what it was that I was potentially going to delegate. The more I knew about it, the more power and leverage I would have as an author.

At that point, it would have been easy to throw in the towel and give up or just wait and see and let things flow. However, I went back to my why and reconnected with the reason why that book meant so much to me. It was the story of my life, living across nine countries, and I wanted it to be a tribute to my late dad, a token of appreciation for the people who have been a part of my life, and a legacy for my daughters so that they can still hear my voice through my stories the day that I'm no longer here. There was no way I was going to let things flow and wait for a potential publisher to maybe take a look at my book and give it a shot. The land of the anti-procrastinator is not a land of ifs, maybes, and waiting. It's a land of action, momentum, initiative, and risks. All those rejections were useful in helping me see and embrace that I needed guidance and support to hone my skills and improve my writing. I underestimated the work required to turn a manuscript into a book people would pay money to read. I also realized that as a new writer who had never published a book before, I could benefit from having a professional assess my work and tell me, with honesty, where I needed to improve and how.

That's when I decided to reach out to a writers' association, the Queensland Writers Centre (QWC), in Australia, to understand how they could help new writers. I was able to see my blind spot (self-awareness), and I was ready to ask for help (vulnerability). The QWC paired me up with Australian bestseller author Vicki Bennett, who would first assess my manuscript and then give me a recommendation based on her insights. I paid the fee, and a few weeks later, after she read the manuscript, we had our initial call. Using kind words, she let me know that my book needed work. 'How much work?' I asked inquisitively. She smiled, paused, elegantly adjusted her glasses, and, with her lovely Aussie accent, replied gently, 'A lot of work, Dear. What you have here is a gem, but it needs polishing. It's currently a manuscript, and we have to turn it into a book. We are talking months, but you will get there, and I'm here to help you.'

Wow. My beloved book needed months of work. I was miles away from the finish line. I thought I had done the heavy lifting, but the real work was just about to start. I took a deep (and less elegant) breath and said with a firm tone, 'Okay, let's do this. Let me know how we move on from here.'

I signed up for a coaching package with Vicki as my mentor. I knew that if I wanted to play in the big league and have a real chance as a writer, I needed to work on my blind spots, become a better writer, and polish my gem. Besides the technical help, I also needed motivation and encouragement to make it to the finish line, an accountability partner who would be supporting me along the way, like the crew that supports the cyclists during the Tour de France. Unlike the vanity publishers, my mentor didn't do anything for me but with me. Vicki guided me in the right direction, gave me pointers to elevate my writing, highlighted the parts of my book that I needed to work on, and praised me for the work that deserved recognition. It was bloody hard and bloody rewarding at the same time.

Every time I emailed her a chapter I had edited and revised, she would send it back with dozens of red comments such as 'Tautology', 'Explain', and 'Irrelevant'. One of my favourite comments of all time from Vicki was, '"Get" is such an inelegant word. Please find a more descriptive term.' She was right. Sometimes, my writing became lazy, and I resorted to the most multitasking English word of all, 'get'. I was procrastinating with my writing.

After reading my own book over ten times to edit it 'just one more time', I was regurgitating my own words. I procrastinated before going through the manuscript review and found dozens of excuses and minor tasks to avoid the big one: polishing my work. However, I had an accountability agreement with my mentor, and that created an extra layer of security, like an additional seatbelt in case of a motivation crash.

When do you need to ask a third person for help? Sometimes, it's not about doing everything alone but having the self-awareness and the vulnerability to admit that we are not skilled enough (yet) and might need a little push or guidance from someone to make things happen. If you are not seeing the results after trying consistently for a sustained period of time, it might be worth partnering with a professional. For instance, if you have been attempting to lose weight by trying different diets for months without success, it might be a good idea to talk to a nutritionist. If you constantly struggle to finish things on time and have a list of unfinished projects, it's worth finding ways to dial up accountability. It could be a mentor or a coach who will keep you on track and cheer you on from the sidelines.

Vicki and I worked hand in hand for around six months from December 2022. When I did the final book review, I was a different writer from when I had started the manuscript, and it was a totally different book. Not only had I become a better writer, but I had also grown as an individual, having gone through the process of rejection, identifying my blind spots, and opening the vulnerability door to let a mentor in with the constructive feedback and criticism it implied. In the process, my overall writing skills improved, and I started to see results. My articles on Medium started to perform better, generating more views and earnings, and my newsletter also started to gain traction, going from one to two new subscribers a day to over twenty, reaching 2,000 in slightly over one year. Seeing that timid spark of success helped reinforce my identity as a writer and my why. My chain of reaction was well and truly in motion, and I had found my way to mitigate resistance by asking for help when I most needed it.

My raw diamond was now starting to shine after a lot of polishing. In September 2023, an independent publisher, Earnshaw Books, took an interest in my book, and shortly after, I signed my first publishing deal. *The Flight Home* was launched in December, and I celebrated with my husband on a romantic date at our favourite French restaurant in Kennedy Town. I kept the promise I had made to myself and to my community to publish my book by the end of the year. Public accountability, self-awareness, and vulnerability helped me defeat procrastination and make a life dream come true. We celebrated not only the book launch but also the journey. I had fought a thousand demons, resisted the temptation to give up a thousand times, and managed to make my dream come true, one page at a time. Yes, I needed a bit of help—hell, yes, a lot of help—and I'm glad I asked for it because sometimes, you do need a little push to cultivate your land. In February 2024, *The Flight Home* was recognized with the Literary Titan Award, my first book award ever.

Regulating Distractions

Procrastination's best friend is called distraction. Ask a bored person to complete the task they have been putting off, and they will literally find ten excuses and random objections. 'I still have time', 'I will get to it', 'I can do it tomorrow'. We all have that tedious task that has been pending for months, that email we dread to send. It's usually something like an RSVP to an event we feel bad about not going to, a boring admin task, a routine health checkup, or anything that our brain puts off, mostly because it's unpleasant or requires too much effort, even if we know it's good for us. It's our nature creating resistance against ourselves and our why.

Ironically, procrastination also goes hand in hand with creativity. Instead of writing the dreaded email, you might start a methodical cleaning of your laptop screen until it's so pristine that you can see your (procrastinating) face on the screen. I even offer my husband a free cleaning service for his Mac just to avoid facing the frog. Instead of sending the RSVP I have been putting off for days, I decide it's the perfect time to rearrange the clothes in my wardrobe in a colour-coded fashion or do the dishes. Instead of making the appointment with the doctor, I decide it's the best time to empty my purse of all the random stuff I find there, from candy packages to taxi receipts, hair bands, a doll shoe . . . Procrastination has the power to trigger creativity, but sadly, that creativity is rather random and has short legs. No Picasso today.

In our digital-first world, distraction can take many different shapes and formats, but it often takes the shape of a screen: a phone, an iPad, a computer, a smartwatch . . . The biggest distraction we have nowadays is the virtual world, a parallel reality that is asking for our attention 24/7 and becomes smarter at getting it every day with all types of temptation: beauty tips, entertainment, gossip, games, hot news, random (cat) videos, and more. Social media is the sugar rush that our brain has become addicted to. We are bombarded with multisensorial notifications, and we love the instant gratification of a *like* after we upload a selfie or a comment after we publish a post. Having unlimited access to technology in our pockets at our fingertips has revolutionized the way we access and digest information: it's on demand anytime, anywhere. Sometimes, you don't even have to make a choice or press a button. AI has already made the choice on your behalf: The algorithms embedded in the apps know you, your patterns, your taste, and your scrolling patterns, and they use it to keep you hooked. Netflix plays the next episode of the series you are watching by default or starts playing something it has selected for you based on your preferences. You don't need to click a single button, and although you only planned to watch one episode, you end up watching two—or three—because it was effortless and you didn't even have to think. Instagram knows exactly the types of reels that will keep you glued to the screen. Your life is on autopilot, and you can't switch off the button. Pleasure is on shelves and on the go. We have more choices, more availability, and more access, and our brain tells us we need more, more, more when, in reality, we need less.

According to a survey from Reviews.org, adults in the US spent an average of four hours and twenty-five minutes a day on their phones in 2023, a 30 per cent increase from the previous year. They also checked their phones an average of 144 times a day.[13] The data doesn't lie. We spend a significant portion of our lives consumed by screens and social media. We think we consume, but we are the ones being consumed. What was created as a tool to help us be more productive and connected has ironically become a barrier to productivity and meaningful connection. Social media makes us less productive and less connected, yet we can't resist it.

---

[13] Alex Kerai, 'Cell Phone Usage Statistics: Mornings Are for Notifications', Reviews.org, 21 July 2023, https://www.reviews.org/mobile/cell-phone-addiction/.

When I ask friends, colleagues, and fellow writers what their number one distraction is, the answer is unanimous: their phone. Whether it's a WhatsApp message, a new email, or a notification, technology creates an illusion of urgency. When you hear a beep or feel the phone ring or the watch vibrate, your brain reacts to it; it's triggered by an alarm. Most notifications and messages can wait until the next break, but we trick ourselves into believing that it might uncover something urgent that requires immediate attention, or we are simply too curious to wait. As a result, we are constantly in reactive mode and in a mental state of permanent alert, reacting to external signals and stimulation. The worst is that we often react before the trigger and reach out to our phone 'just to check', even if there is no notification.

When I talk to my husband, I refer to social media as the rabbit hole. This is usually how it goes: I have to fill out a tedious form for my daughter's school, but while I'm online, I decide to quickly check Facebook. I see I have five new notifications, and the mental sugar rush hits me and creates a sense of urgency. *Those notifications can't wait and must be seen right now; it's only a few seconds anyway.* So, I click on the digital bell and see that one is a reminder about a friend's birthday. I realize I had forgotten about it and quickly jump to WhatsApp to send her a happy birthday message. And while I'm on WhatsApp, I see other unread messages that also need immediate attention. One of them is about a dinner on Thursday night that I need to confirm, and I start thinking about my week and check my calendar app. Eventually, I get distracted and slip into a procrastination elevator that was triggered by one external signal. This vicious cycle goes on and on from app to app, and by the end of the day, I have easily spent over four hours on and off social media and apps, disrupting my productivity. As per the school form, I never managed to fill it out that day because I then moved on to something else until I inadvertently missed the deadline. Now, I have to write to the school apologizing and sending the form that I could have sent days ago. Does this pattern sound familiar?

Now, imagine if out of those three hours you spend browsing through social media daily, you dedicated 50 per cent to being productive and getting things done. What if you suddenly had an extra couple of hours in your day, your week, and your life to do more things, whether it's more time to focus on work, leisure, or learning a new skill? Not only that, imagine if, during the time dedicated to working, you were fully focused without interruption, without message alerts, and flashing screens. How much more productive and fulfilled would you be?

Productivity experts and mindfulness coaches unanimously emphasize the importance of focus. It's not about working more but optimizing the time available to produce, create, and ideate without being pulled in different directions. It's about reaching the state of full clarity, a state of flow. It's about quality time.

At the end of 2023, I decided I had enough of being dependent on my phone. I had created an unhealthy routine around technology that turned it from a tool into an addiction. The first thing I would do in the morning was check my phone. The last thing I would do before turning off the lights in bed was check my phone. I would browse through LinkedIn on my phone while walking my dog; I would put my phone on the table by default while having dinner with my husband; I had my phone next to my laptop at all times while working and every five or ten minutes, I would do the rounds, like a doctor, patrolling the social media corridors: LinkedIn, Medium, Substack, WhatsApp . . . and then I would go back to my duty. Except that I was not the doctor here; I was the patient who needed to be more focused, less distracted, more present, and less withdrawn. I was starting to slip into the dangerous territory of addiction and burnout, and I needed to be here and now, in the moment.

I tried different things to minimize the use of my phone while I was working. I put it in a different room; I limited the screen time per day; I put a time cap on the various apps; I started to leave the phone at home when I was doing things such as walking my dog or exercising. I also turned off the notifications on my Apple Watch as it was constantly vibrating. All these measures had a remarkable impact on my productivity as well as my well-being, but it was still not enough. Then something happened . . .

One weekend in December 2023, I went camping with my husband and our daughters. We left early on a Saturday morning and took a taxi to the Saikung Pier in the New Territories in Hong Kong. Once there, we all hopped on a small wooden motorboat called Sampan that took us to a stunning and secluded beach, forty minutes away, called Tai Long Wan. As we arrived at the beach, we carried our backpacks and walked on the warm sand towards a spot in the shade to set up our tents. Once we agreed on our camping location for the night, I checked my phone and noticed it had no connectivity bars. I lifted it with my hands, moving it in different directions while pointing at the sky, but there was no cellular connection. It was just us and nature. I confess I initially felt disappointed and slightly anxious. *What if I miss something?* Being disconnected from the world for twenty-four hours seemed like a long time. I put the phone on the foldable table and started unpacking, organizing the food, and preparing for the beach day. The girls played tag and looked for treasures buried in the sand. Dave and I teamed up to set up the tent (he did most of the work), and when it was ready, we sat down on a beach towel and had a glass of wine, watching our daughters throw shells and dig holes in the sand. We chatted about our plans for the new year. We talked about finances, trips, fitness, races, work . . . And then we stayed there in silence, soaking in the beauty of the moment: the light breeze, the wintery sun that was still warm enough to comfort our skin, the chirrup of the birds, and the feeling of being present in the present.

When the night arrived, we started preparing a BBQ. Dave lit up a fire with coal and some dry branches he had collected in the afternoon with the girls. We prepared burgers and sausages, but the highlight of the dinner was, of course, the marshmallows on sticks. We kissed the girls goodnight, and I didn't check my phone as I always did before going to bed. When I woke up in the morning before dawn, my instinct was to reach out to my phone to check the messages across the ten different apps, but then I remembered

I didn't have any connection, so I left it inside the tent and went to make a cup of coffee instead. It hadn't even been one full day without technology, and I was already feeling so much more present and engaged. All my senses were engaged. I felt alive and free. I thought I was disconnected from the world when, in reality, I reconnected with the real world without interruptions for the first time in a long while. Once back home, I thought I would be less productive because I hadn't been on my phone 'keeping up with life', but the opposite happened: I had new ideas (creativity), I had focus (clarity), and I was able to do better work with fewer interruptions (productivity). The trifecta.

The camping trip was an eye-opener about the negative impact technology and social media were having on me and my life, but it also opened a door to new possibilities. Things didn't have to be that way; technology didn't have to be a distraction. I had the option of being in control and using social media as a tool versus becoming its tool. I decided that my very simple math for success was more focus, more clarity, and more mindfulness, and the best way to action the formula was to eliminate distractions. I didn't need to add more hours sitting in front of my laptop; I didn't need to give up time with my family; I didn't need to find more hours in the day; I needed to be intentional about those hours and find the flow again, free from distractions, and make every hour count, turning time into my ally.

The idea of reducing the usage of my phone and particularly social media to a bare minimum started tempting me since the camping trip. However, with international travelling and the Christmas holidays in between, I didn't implement any measures until mid-January 2024. I didn't have a specific date planned in my calendar, but one afternoon, as I caught myself staring at my phone one more time while I was playing with my daughters, I decided that that was it. I had cold feet and deleted social media from my phone. Not just Band-Aid solutions like limiting my daily usage, turning on the black-and-white mode, or putting the phone in the room next door. I decided to remove all the social media apps from my phone and eliminate temptation from my pocket. I deleted not only

Facebook and Instagram but also apps that I use for work, such as LinkedIn, Medium, and Substack. I wanted to have a clear distinction between my work and my personal time, so I decided that social media would only happen during work hours on my laptop.

Wow, that felt radical, daunting, and liberating at the same time. I felt both super disconnected and super connected: disconnected from the virtual world and the sugar rush from the notifications but connected to the present, with the present, in the present. I thought it was going to be impossible to be off social media for hours, particularly in my line of work where I create content daily across various platforms and receive dozens of notifications and messages. Surprisingly, you don't miss what you don't have, and the human brain is extremely adaptable and adjusts to new habits and surroundings in a matter of days.

On day two, I felt strange and alienated. I pulled my phone by default multiple times, only to realize there was nothing to check. By day three, I wasn't checking my phone in the morning, and by day four, I even took my time when I woke up to have my coffee and do my stretch session before checking social media on my Mac. After only a week, the results were astonishing. I checked the data on my iPhone—my screen time had gone down by 37 per cent to two hours and forty-nine minutes daily, compared to four to five hours previously. My new screen time usage was split between email and WhatsApp, the main tools I use for communication on the go. I also had some time on finance apps and on Strava, the app I use daily to record my workouts and keep track of my fitness. If there was anything urgent, people could call me or message me. It was a transformational change in my approach to technology and a radical change in my lifestyle. Suddenly, I had an extra fifteen hours a week! Additionally, the work I was doing was more focused because I could be writing for an hour without being distracted by notifications or my phone. I was able to find my flow.

Time is your most valuable resource. It's limited, scarce, and can't be replaced: You can't buy the five hours you wasted today. That time is gone. Every person has a different understanding of what value means: For me, browsing aimlessly on social media is time wasted, but watching thirty minutes of Bluey, my daughters' favourite cartoon show, as a family on the couch after we have finished the workday and homework is a lovely activity that brings me joy and pleasure. You are your best judge, and deep down, you know your demons and the things that keep you from focusing on what really matters. For many, it's the phone, particularly social media. If they have it within reach, they are constantly checking notifications or finding excuses to grab it and get into an app. Know your rabbit hole and own it so that you can be in control. Time magically increases when you use it intentionally and eliminate distractions. One hour of focused, uninterrupted work is gold in the digital age. Dig deep and find your gold.

Exercise

List your top distractions and try to quantify how much time you spend on them every day. For phone usage, you can check the screen time in your device settings, the exact hours and minutes you spend every week, and where those hours go.

Set a specific goal for reducing those hours with specific actions to help you reach it.

For example, 'I spend four hours and thirty minutes every day on my phone, and I want to reduce it to two hours. I'm going to put the phone away while I'm working and only check it during the breaks.'

The Accountability Mirror

As emphasized earlier, humans tend to procrastinate when there is a choice. If you have two months to study for the exam, you can afford to procrastinate; however, when you only have forty-eight hours left, the procrastination window becomes narrower and narrower. Time abundance is often the best excuse for procrastination: You can delay the project, start tomorrow, or take five more minutes, and you will still be fine.

On the flip side, time can also be used to fight procrastination. If you don't have a timeline, create one; if you don't have a tight deadline, fabricate it yourself. Establish your own calendar and turn curfews into your allies. A good old mentor once challenged me to delete the term 'ASAP' from my vocabulary and my emails. He explained that ASAP is as good as my guess or his: it's subjective and abstract and doesn't carry any responsibility. It can mean immediately for you but twenty-four hours for somebody else. It's a way of demonstrating an intention without making a commitment, a non-binding agreement to make you feel good. That conversation happened five years before I wrote this book, and I have never used the term ASAP again. If you want things to happen, put an expiration date on them and show it on your calendar. Announce your curfew on the loudspeakers and create your own sense of urgency.

When I was discussing the terms for this book with my publisher, Nora, she asked me how long I needed to write the manuscript and submit the first draft. We had already agreed that the approximate word count was going to be 60,000 words. I did a quick calculation of the average words I can commit to per day, and based on my estimation and a buffer for editing, I set the time frame myself: ninety days after signing the contract. It was an ambitious time frame: short enough to create an imminent sense of urgency and keep me focused but long enough to allow me to complete it following a rigorous plan. If I had set a timeline of six months instead of three, I'm convinced it would have taken me six months to write it. This is known as Parkinson's Law, according to which, our work expands to fit in the time we allocate to it. We are creatures of comfort, and if we have twice the time to complete a task, we usually take twice as long. No one is immune to the Parkinson's Law, however, we can overwrite it by creating our own (anti-procrastination) laws and artificially manipulating timelines to our advantage to increase productivity. Don't fear tight deadlines: leverage them to succeed.

This rationale was partly inspired by Elon Musk and his unorthodox way of running his businesses, eloquently explained by Walter Isaacson in Musk's latest biography. Across all his companies, from Tesla to SpaceX and Neuralink, Musk uses the same leadership approach for his team and for himself: He sets extremely ambitious timelines to accomplish targets. His team would often complain at first and call him insane (and other names), but after the initial pushback, they would rally the troops to push themselves, turn on the turbo, and perform. The result, more often than not, was that they either achieved the unachievable targets or they got pretty close in the process. It was a simple equation: if they took more shots and pushed themselves harder against the clock, chances were they would score more shots. And they did. Whether Musk's radical approach works or doesn't work for you doesn't matter. What's important to keep in mind is that things that don't have a date in the calendar are less likely to happen than those that do. ASAP doesn't mean anything, and 'one day' is a cushioned euphemism for never.

If you plan to write a book, set a timeline. For my memoir, in January 2023, I decided to announce to my connections on social media that I was going to publish it by the end of the year. I wanted to build accountability with others but more so with myself. Had I not had a timeline, I might have delayed the launch, especially as I had the editing crisis to deal with. I selected 8 December as the go-live date because the number 8 represents fortune and good luck in Chinese, as it sounds similar to the character for prosperity. When the lucky date was approaching, and we were still finalizing the details of the launch, the publisher gave me the option to postpone the publishing for a few days or even weeks. There was no penalty and no major implications. The procrastinator in me whispered, 'Take your time; don't rush things; enjoy the holidays and launch the book in the new year.' It sounded tempting. However, by having set a date, I wanted to keep my word and make things happen on my terms. I didn't want to let myself down and break my promise to others and to myself. Also, I had strategically planned that date before Christmas to time it with the spike in book sales during the holidays, and I didn't want to miss out on the opportunity of being a holiday release on Amazon and in the bookstores.

The Flight Home went live on 8 December, and I was over the moon to deliver on my word, see my hard work pay off, and turn my life story into a published book. I removed every ASAP, and by doing so, I established my own curfew and fabricated urgency, turning one day into day one.

Setting a timeline is not only about being specific but also strategic, picking a date that adds an extra layer of urgency, such as your birthday, a life event, the beginning of a new year, or a key marketing moment. You might want to launch a fitness guide just before summer to encourage people to get bikini fit. You might hire a coach to work on your presentation skills before a big keynote or your first TEDx talk. If you want to transform the way you look, celebrate the 2.0 version of yourself in your calendar, like my friend Ana did. If someone invites you to speak on a podcast, don't leave the invitation open. Book the session in the calendar and make things happen.

Whenever possible, set a date for the next step, the next call, or the next appointment, especially for things that generate anxiety or apprehension. These usually involve unpleasant customer conversations, tedious admin tasks, reports, a dentist or doctor appointment, and things that make us step out of our comfort zone. The newsletter that you are planning to launch, the podcast you want to speak on, and the book you said you were going to write 'one day' suddenly become real when you materialize them into a date.

If you have one month to write a report, you do it in one month. If you have one week, you do it in one week. And if you only have one day, you do it in one day. It's the law of procrastination, whereby low accountability leads to high procrastination, and high accountability leads to low procrastination. Again, you procrastinate because you can, but the moment you become accountable, you shut down the procrastination window.

Accountability can be created through different channels and mechanisms with higher or lower levels of commitment, which vary from an agreement with a friend to a public announcement on social media or even a legal obligation. Below are some mechanisms for creating accountability that can work in isolation or in combination.

The Accountability Buddy

This system works when the individuals involved share a common goal and are committed to it (running, losing weight, quitting smoking, writing, studying . . .). That common identity creates a mutually beneficial commitment where both parties are compelled to deliver, or else they fall behind. Having a regular check-in process helps to keep motivation alive. Think of group chats dedicated to fitness and exercise, where friends share updates of the progress and pictures, or signing up for a six-week detox programme with your best friend.

In my sports circle, we keep each other accountable by announcing our racing goals and giving updates on our training. Interestingly, the motivation of two people is greater when combined, and the sum becomes larger than its parts. Very often, all it takes is one friend to sign up for a race to have half the team follow.

Building in Public

Public accountability is effective because it creates a deep sense of responsibility towards others and towards yourself, like I shared in the example above. The level of exposure can vary, depending on whether it's your close circle of friends, your peers, your social network, or your broader community. Most likely, people won't remember your public announcement and goals, but the point is, *you will*, and that's what matters. The bigger the exposure, the bigger the accountability. You can start sharing your goals with your friends and family, and take it one step further and announce it on your social media channels.

I always share my goals with my community on LinkedIn and my newsletter subscribers. Writing the targets down helps to materialize them and make them real; sharing them with the public adds an extra layer of accountability.

Creating Urgency

In the previous pages, we saw how lack of urgency is one of the key self-reported reasons behind procrastination. The solution is simple:

shorten the time frames. Try twenty-four hours, one week, or one month to create a sense of urgency. Fabricate your own curfews to make things happen.

When you have an option, take the first available booking: a podcast invite, a doctor's appointment, a business meeting . . . Be ready to be ready!

Putting the Money on the Table

No one likes to throw cash away, and money can be a powerful accountability driver. Whenever you sign up for a coach, a gym membership, or purchase an entry ticket, you significantly increase the chances of that event happening. Whenever I hesitate to do something I already paid for, I force myself to visualize that money being thrown in the bin.

When I paid USD 1,000 to the Queensland Writers Centre for the mentoring package, I knew I was going to publish my book. When I paid the entry fee for the Ironman, I knew I would show up at the jetty in Busselton, Australia, ready for the sufferfest. I had put my money on the table, and my name was on the starters' list. Will moves mountains, but money puts the foot on the accelerator.

Accountability kills procrastination. Become your own accountability buddy and make things happen.

From Accountability to Action

One of the common features of successful people is their bias for action. Entrepreneurs, in particular, are constantly testing, failing, adjusting, and innovating. They don't avoid risks; they mitigate them and keep going. They will fail fourteen out of fifteen times, but statistics are in their favour. They will discover fourteen ways that don't work, only to discover the one that does. More shots, more wins. That's the mindset that will help you start things and do them better every time.

By nature, individuals have different levels of risk tolerance, and the threshold also varies depending on the nature of the event.

Dave, for instance, is much more risk-prone than I am when it comes to finances and investment decisions. While he is very active in cryptocurrency and is comfortable with the volatility that comes with it, I'm more conservative and prefer to invest in more stable assets such as real estate or tech stock. That makes us a good team: I'm always the one raising the red flag for potential risks and losses, and he's the one pushing me to take more risks.

On the other hand, doing things that I have never done before is something that doesn't scare me, or if it does, I turn that anxiety into excitement and motivation. The way I cultivate a bias for action is by focusing on the impact rather than the action itself or the result. The impact always leads to the same destination: personal growth. Whether you do a great job and build confidence in that particular skill, or it's a disaster and learn from your mistakes, doing new things is always an opportunity to grow.

A bias for action means that you are going to fail significantly more than the average person who doesn't embrace risk and only takes calculated steps within their comfort zone. The good thing is that you also become much more comfortable with failure and learn to reframe it as growth. The more you get out of your comfort zone, the bigger your comfort zone gets. There's no failing if you decide to learn from it; there's only failing forward.

In January 2023, my friend and personal brand strategist Petra and I decided we were going to launch a LinkedIn Live series to talk about building authority online and investing in a personal brand. Neither of us had ever hosted such sessions before, and we had no idea how to handle the technology, host the Live session, and market it to the public. Being action-driven, we both decided to set a live date two weeks later and figure out what we needed to do to make the session happen. After creating an account on the streaming platform StreamYard and doing a test run, we created the marketing assets on Canva and announced the event on LinkedIn. On the day of the live session, we were both nervous wrecks thinking about all the things that could go wrong: technical issues, mental blackout, falling short on content . . . We then reframed our mindset and turned all those risks into a learning opportunity. Instead of focusing on what could go wrong, we focused on what could go well: connecting with people, having exposure, building credibility and confidence in front of the camera, and the experience of doing something for the first time. In the worst-case scenario, attendees would drop the session, and we would end up having a public coffee chat with a camera on.

Developing a bias for action is challenging, especially for people with a more conservative nature. A great way to practice it is by creating a safe environment where the risk is cushioned and mitigated, like when I go bowling, and I put the bumpers for my daughters (and for myself). Hosting a live session on LinkedIn was a relatively safe environment for testing the waters. Although the event was live and public, there was no legal commitment with the audience, and it was free of charge. In case the session turned out to be a disaster, we might receive a couple of negative comments and perhaps lose some followers. Nothing tragic. I wouldn't try (or recommend) a live session for the first time with a paid cohort, for instance. Use the bumpers first to build confidence while honing the skill, and remove them once you are ready to go for the full strike.

The best way to encourage action is to create a protected trial-and-error environment where mistakes are tolerated and have minimum repercussions. This allows one to practice and improve while minimizing the risks. The worst-case scenario should be bearable and carry minor consequences. The benefits from the lessons and the practice should outdo the risks of failure.

Focus on your first step as a goal, no matter how small and unimpressive that step might seem. Write the first page of your new book; aim to go for your first jog; book your first appointment with your coach or personal trainer. Once there is action, it becomes easier to create momentum and remember that every marathon starts with one first step.

Summary

- Your formula for an optimal productivity routine is and must be unique. There isn't a one-size-fits-all manual, which means you must write your own and keep iterating through trial and error.
- The most effective remedies to combat procrastination come from a place of honesty and self-awareness. You must be willing to look in the vulnerability mirror, acknowledge both your weaknesses and your blind spots, and act on them to seal the cracks.
- If you want your land to be the most productive, you must look inward and master self-regulation emotionally, physically, and mentally. However, you must also look outward and regulate your external environment to create a conducive space and a routine that sets you up for success, eliminating distractions and doubling down on accountability.

4

FINDING YOUR TRIBE

Your Direct Circle

Your environment has a huge impact on your life. Your external environment impacts your health; exposure to the sun and humidity impacts your skin; pollution damages your lungs while clean air purifies them. Every day, you make thousands of decisions based on your surroundings and how they affect you. You apply sunscreen to mitigate the damage from the UV, you try to drink two litres of water to stay hydrated, and you might try to avoid places where you know the pollution is high and the traffic is bad.

Something similar happens with the people you surround yourself with and your social habitat. Humans are made of energy, and some people replenish our tank while others drain us, leaving us spent and depleted. If you spend a day with a person who is genuinely positive and uplifting, you end up feeding off that energy and emanating it. On the other hand, we all know those negative people who always see the glass half empty and find every opportunity to complain. If you spend too much time around them, you end up carrying that same bad juju and intoxicating yourself. Who you spend your time with has a direct correlation and influence on your emotional and mental well-being, your motivation, and, ultimately, your performance and productivity. Energy is contagious.

It's well-known that when sports teams play at home, their chances of winning increase significantly, even though it's the same team with the same players and the same coach. Yet, being at home, surrounded and supported by their people, plays on their psyche and helps them to build the confidence to win. In basketball, NBA teams win 62.7 per cent of their home games. [. . .] International cricket teams win 60.1 per cent of home games. In rugby, the win rate for home teams is 58 per cent, while in American football, it's 57.6 per cent. This is known as the home-field advantage in the sports world.[14]

To a certain degree, your social and emotional entourage precondition your success or at least play a part in it. We all need a positive and supportive space to blossom, and it's easier to do so when people are cheering for us on the sidelines, filling our stadium with words of encouragement, and handing us water bottles as we run our life marathon or sometimes even running it together. Understanding the impact others have on you is critical to building a win-win tribe where people support each other unconditionally and grow together as a result. It sounds obvious, but millions of people spend years in unhappy relationships, toxic workplaces, and friendships that bring them down. They keep the anchors down for so long that they actually forget how to sail and stall in life, like a caged bird that forgets it has wings to fly and, therefore, forgets how to fly.

Do the people around you push you to rise, or do they drag you down?

Do they uplift you and motivate you to achieve your dreams, or do they hold you back by cutting your wings?

The real test happens when you try to do something new, create a new version of yourself, and take a risk. Many people are resistant to change, whether it's a change in the circumstances or in those around them. Particularly if you are stepping out of the common comfort zone, many of those who stay behind, caged in the circle of complacency, struggle to support your efforts and resist the new

---

[14] Nathan Pinger, 'Home Field Advantage: The Facts and the Fiction', *Chicago Booth Review*, 15 June 2015, https://www.chicagobooth.edu/review/home-field-advantage-facts-and-fiction.

identity you are painting with your brush. Change is uncomfortable and always leads to disruption and sometimes friction. Peer pressure is real, and it can be either positive or negative, but there is usually some type of pressure in either direction.

Your direct circle is the people you spend most of your time with and who know you the best. It might be your partner, parents, or close friends. When you are trying to disrupt things and create change in your life, their support is critical, particularly emotionally. Even if they don't understand the technical aspects of what you are trying to achieve, their endorsement and belief in you are precious. You need them to buy into your identity too. However, getting the blessing from the people closest to you can often prove the most challenging because they are often the ones more vested in you. If you have successfully climbed up the corporate ladder for years and decide you now want to venture into unchartered territory, change careers, or start a new path, they might warn you against the risks and encourage you to reconsider and play safe. If you dream too high and aim to reach the A league, they might bring you down to earth and cut your wings because they are trying to protect you from failing and manage your expectations. Sometimes, they might question your decision because they failed when they tried themselves or didn't have the courage to try to start with.

In an ideal world, you want everybody on board, betting for the person you aspire to become. In the real world, it's likely to be a mixed bag. Some people might be reluctant and cynical, especially at first. Others might be hesitant, and a small group will be enthusiastic and 100 per cent behind you. The best way to conquer people's hearts is to make them part of your vision and your journey. Imagine that you are setting off on a sailing expedition, and instead of telling your people about it, you take them along. You show them the destination, the map, and the plan and even invite them to play a role. They become active participants in your adventure.

In practice, this can take many different shapes, and it's up to you and your creativity to design a scenario where you create partners and allies. If you are trying to make a positive change in your lifestyle, such as losing weight, getting fit, or quitting a bad habit like smoking or drinking alcohol, it's the perfect opportunity to bring your best friend or your partner along and row that boat together. Doing things as a couple or a team is much more fun and rewarding, and you build complicity and allyship not only for that specific goal but beyond, in your relationship, because you are evolving together, cementing a shared identity. Start from your common goal, your North Star, and build a joint plan to lose weight, exercise, or give up drinking together. Dave and I always encourage each other to exercise in the morning, go to bed early, and have healthier habits in general. Our shared values (in this case, well-being) allow us to collectively reinforce our identity and implement the behaviours that cement it, such as exercising, drinking more water and less alcohol, and doing our stretching routine together. By being on the same page, we inspire each other, and procrastination doesn't stand a chance against us as a team because two people are stronger at fighting resistance than one.

Not everyone in your circle is going to share all your life goals, and it's unrealistic for you to share theirs. However, you can still find ways to bring them on board, and the best way to do so is by taking them to the backstage of what you are building and giving them a sneak peek into your dream. When I first told my mum and my sister that I was done with the corporate world and was going to start writing and doing public speaking, they were both surprised and hesitant. I was forty-one at the time and had always worn my corporate badge with pride, working in senior leadership roles for Fortune 500 companies. Mum was worried about the financial side, as starting a new venture as a solopreneur from zero was a big risk, especially in an ultra-saturated space such as writing and a very niche field like motivational speaking, where only a few manage to cut through the clutter. My sister, Vicky, thought it was a bit crazy, and she supported me but without fully understanding what I was doing.

From day one, I brought Mum and Vicky to my backstage. I invited them into my sailing boat and asked them to help me lift the anchors. I shared my first articles with them and celebrated the small wins, such as speaking on my first podcast or publishing my first book. I gave them a front seat and showed them everything I was creating. I was candid about my frustration when publishers rejected me. They were the first to see my book covers, and I shared with them the deals for public speaking I had won and lost. I made them my support team and my Tour de France crew, and by showing them the behind-the-scenes, they not only saw the outcome but were also part of the production. They celebrated the wins with me and helped me broadcast them in their own circles, and they also comforted me when things didn't go well. They followed my journey online, going from no followers to a community of 20,000 spread across multiple platforms. Although they were not in Hong Kong for my first book signing event in October 2023, they were the first people I sent the video to, and they lived the moment with me from the other side of the world. They didn't understand everything I was doing, but they knew enough to be convinced that I was living my dream, putting my heart and soul into it, and waking up excited every day to build my career as a writer and public speaker.

It's not easy to win people's hearts and genuine endorsements, but that's not a reason not to try. Always start with the vision, your why, and your values, and aim to inspire your partner, family, and friends with it. The more they understand what you do and especially why you do it, the more likely they are to jump on board and help you put up the sails. For some people, it might take longer; others might jump on board straightaway, but never assume that just because it's your dream, everybody is going to be cheering for you from day one. You have to make it easy for them and be the translator to help them connect the dots. Invite them to the backstage and make them active players in your adventure. You need the support from those close to you.

The Anchors

Sadly, many people around you struggle when you start something new and turn your dream into action. You often hear stories of friendships that break when one person takes a new path and decides to break away from the pack. Change always disrupts the flow and opens the door for questions and discomfort, and not everyone is ready for that.

My friend Alia had a conventional upbringing in Spain. She grew up in a small city called Valladolid, went to a Catholic school, and graduated from law school. She had her circle of friends from primary school, all with a similar background and education. They were like-minded girls from like-minded families who liked to party on the weekends and spend the summer holidays in the same beach destinations along the Mediterranean coast. Growing up, their life had been similar, following conventional standards and tradition. However, in her early twenties, Alia decided to apply for a student scholarship called Erasmus in order to finish her last year of law school in Bologna, Italy. I obtained the same scholarship, and that's how I met her at a students' dorm party, and we instantly clicked. Back then, Alia only spoke Spanish and some English, but she was keen to experience and explore the world outside of her hometown and learn a new culture and language. She was the only one among her friends to have an international experience beyond spending a couple of weeks in the UK in the summer to learn English.

Alia soon made friends from many different nationalities: French, Germans, Greeks, and, of course, Italians. Her experience in Bologna was an eye-opener about the possibilities the world offered outside the confines of Valladolid. She was meeting interesting people with different life stories and cultures, and she found it fascinating. She spent a fantastic year during which she didn't study much, but she enriched herself by visiting the famous towns around Bologna, such as Padova, Ravenna, and Rimini. She learned to speak Italian and improved her English at the same time. She dated interesting men from different countries and discovered a new passion for travelling and learning from other cultures—not as a tourist, like she used to in the past, but as an insider. Her international experience had just started, and she was hungry for more. After she finished a master's in human resources in Madrid, she set off on her journey around the globe. She spent a few months in Malta, learning English, which happened to be a very bad idea because people in Malta don't really speak fluent English. She moved to Malaysia for a job opportunity and spent a year as a consultant in Kuala Lumpur. Although she found it hard to adapt to the local culture and make friends, she made the most of the Asian experience and continued growing, learning, and travelling. She then spent a few months in Jordan, where her dad's family was originally from, to reconnect with her roots and her Jordan cousins and study Arabic. Eventually, she settled down in Abu Dhabi, UAE, after years of adventures and memories spread around the world. I visited Alia on holiday in every place she once called home, and every time we met, she was more confident and accomplished. She had embraced the positives each culture had to offer and had been able to adjust and create her happiness no matter where she was.

Alia went from being inside the mould to breaking the mould altogether and creating her own colourful shape. Her interests changed as she discovered the world. She started to thrive both personally and professionally and made new friends from all parts of the world. Her identity evolved around the principles of culture and curiosity and her chain of reaction took her to places, both literally and figuratively. She spread her wings like a bright and colourful bird and blossomed into a fascinating woman who was confident and was able to light up a room the moment she walked in.

Back in her hometown, things were different. Every time she went back home on holiday to visit her family and friends, she would feel a bit more disconnected and out of sync. At first, her old school friends seemed interested in what she was doing and her experience overseas. It was exciting and exotic, just like a new summer destination. However, as soon as the novelty had worn off, they would default to their old topics, usual conversations, and gossip about people in their network. Whenever Alia talked about her experience abroad and her life overseas, her friends would often deviate from the conversation or just let it run its course without much interest and input. Sometimes, they would make jokes, calling her posh and Miss Glamour. It was always with humour, but there was a hint of truth, and Alia often felt left out. She was different; she had changed and struggled to find her place in her old world where change was not welcome.

That's when Alia would subconsciously go back to her old self, tie her wings, and adjust to fit in. There was little room for growth, and she felt suffocated as much as her friends felt overwhelmed and intimidated by her adventurous life. She had to mask and avoid sharing too much about her life and her travels because there was no understanding, and her friends couldn't relate to something so foreign and, in their minds, unattainable. Some were perhaps jealous because they had never had the courage to leave their town and live a wild adventure. Others simply had no interest in expanding their horizons to appreciate a life different from theirs, but above all, they disliked change. In their mind, they had lost a part of their friend who was no longer 'like them' and they were not ready to let go of the confines of the only world they had ever known.

Unsurprisingly, when Alia got married years later, none of her old friends attended her wedding party in Abu Dhabi. Instead, she had dozens of new friends who had travelled from all the corners of the world to celebrate her special day and be part of her tribe as she was sailing to a new destination.

When you reinvent yourself, you challenge the way things are and the social logic and open a new reality not only for yourself but also for those around you. They, too, are dealing with your change. And the closer they are to you, the more they are exposed to it because they feel the ripple effects first-hand.

When I started my new career as a solopreneur in 2022, I dropped the corporate ladder and began writing and building my personal brand on LinkedIn. I then had a very small network, and most were former colleagues, acquaintances, and people who knew me from my previous life in the corporate world. Back then, I didn't have a clear strategy for how I was going to use the platform, but I was willing to take a risk and start building a name for myself, share my thoughts in public, and advocate for causes that matter to me. I started posting about growth mindset, culture, well-being, and a wide variety of topics, from leadership to inclusion. As someone who had never shared anything with strangers online other than my new jobs, whenever I updated my career status, it was a big change. I started posting, sharing ideas and selfies, and commenting on other people's posts and articles. Shortly after that, I also started speaking in public. I spoke on my first podcast as a guest in August 2022, and since then, I started giving interviews and joining other podcasts monthly, sometimes even weekly. I didn't realize it at the time, but looking back and zooming out, it was a 180-degree transformation. I went from being a spectator and having no voice in the digital world to making it my office, my networking space, my business incubator, and everything in between. I started to post daily and published dozens of articles and interviews, building a personal brand in alignment with my values. It was a reinvention, especially for someone over forty who was supposed to have everything figured out by then. I had nothing figured out but I had lifted my anchors and was sailing in the direction I had set. The navigation wasn't always smooth, and I felt lost many times, but I felt liberated, empowered, and free. I had full ownership of my life canvas and was ready to create my new identity, one stroke at a time.

However, very often, I would have conversations with friends or connections that would leave me flat, hesitant, and full of insecurities. Some would say things like, 'So, are you an influencer now?' Others projected themselves into my journey, 'I could never expose myself in public like that,' or would joke that I was becoming someone else, 'You are the new x.'

In reality, I was just me and still me, but a better version of myself or at least a new one that I was keen to explore. I never knew the intent behind those comments. They most probably didn't have the intention to hurt me, but they acted as heavyweights holding me back. Just like Alia, I would sometimes feel embarrassed after catching up with friends and hearing those comments, particularly in larger groups, and felt I had to justify myself. I didn't want the attention or criticism. I didn't want people to project their own judgment onto my dream. I just wanted them to support what I was doing because that was *my* dream, and I was working hard towards it.

Those same people who seemed to know everything about what I was building seldom bothered to support my work in public, read my books, or leave a word of encouragement. Yet, many had an opinion about what I should or shouldn't do, how I should niche or diversify, how I should post less frequently or write a book about x. I had the sad realization that many people around me were pulling me down, just like when, fifteen years earlier, I had become a triathlete, and my party friends would call me obsessed and boring and warn me I was getting too muscular.

I was clear on my chain of reaction and my new identity as a public speaker and author, but many around me were uncomfortable with my 2.0 version. I was supposed to be a corporate girl who was quietly climbing up the corporate ladder and living the hustle life like I had done for years, just like everybody else. Instead, I was taking risks, defying conventional thinking, and creating my own crazy path, following my passion. They didn't understand this different type of hustle, and they didn't like what they didn't understand and, therefore, rejected it. As a result, I avoided bringing up anything that had to do with my public work in conversations and stopped sharing the good news and milestones when they happened. Some would eventually find out through social media and congratulate me, but for many, it was a quick conversation to brush under the carpet and move on. They were not ready to be part of my sailing crew and see beyond the only destination they had ever known.

When you are trying to change, take on a new challenge, and create a new reality, you shake things and unlock disruption. You break the flow for yourself but also for those in your circle, and it leads to questions, discomfort, and sometimes rupture. You are breaking the status quo with a what-if that can be confronting. Some people need time to cope and embrace that new reality, while others will never jump on board. Whether it's a reflection of their own insecurities and frustrations or just a lack of growth mindset and adaptability, the outcome is that they create resistance in your journey, and they will slow you down or even sabotage your adventure. They are the people who are pushing the same door you are trying to open, but they are going in the opposite direction. It's important to understand what role each person plays in your development and what impact, positive or negative, they have on you. Sometimes, you must lift the anchors in order to keep sailing.

The Sails

While some people act as brakes and slow down or even boycott your navigation efforts, others act as lifts and sails. These are the people you want around you day in and day out. They are the voices that will help you reinforce your beliefs and accelerate your chain of reaction. That is the tribe you want to be a part of. Your tribe.

Especially when you have set your intention and have taken your first step or are about to, that's when you need your crew the most. The first step is always the hardest. It's not easy to drag yourself out of the couch if you have been sedentary for years and decide to go to the gym for the first time. It's not easy to publish your first post online and be exposed to thousands of strangers on the internet. It's not easy to go live on your first podcast, wondering how you will come across on the other side of the screen. The first step defines a before and an after, and that's when you need the helping hand, the kind words, and the cheering on the sidelines. You need your crew around you, just like when you are doing a triathlon and a stranger shouts your name while you are running, and it gives you a motivational boost.

Creating your cheerleading squad will help you get a lift when you are starting, a hug when you are feeling down, and a high-five when you cross the finish line. As you put together your tribe, you will find out that there are three main types of people who can support you along your journey, both directly and indirectly.

Your Peers

First, you can look into your new group of peers. These are people on a similar journey to yours. They share the common goal of getting fit, becoming an entrepreneur, or doing something for the first time. Even if you don't have a strong bond to start with and come from different backgrounds and walks of life, there is a strong sense of camaraderie and empathy when people embark on a similar adventure. A shared vision brings people together. Mums-to-be bond together because they want to be the best mothers they possibly can be, and they share a new identity as future parents. New entrepreneurs find common ground in the thrill of building something new and monetizing an idea. Triathlon beginners instantly click because they share the same insecurities, challenges, and goals. You are learning how to ride a triathlon bike, how to transition from the run to the ride, and how to manage your nutrition on race day. Humans relate to each other through values, challenges, and passions, basically through shared identities; and when those materialize, they turn into experiences: a race together, a business partnership, or becoming a parent, for example.

Whatever you are trying to achieve, it's important to pause and identify who your peers are, where they are, and how you can connect with them and support each other. When I joined my triathlon club in Hong Kong, I quickly bonded with a group of girls. We all had different backgrounds and jobs and came from different countries. The one thing we had in common was our new shared identity as triathlon rookies. We were new in that world, and we were learning to combine three sports in one. Being with other people who were in the same boat and had the same silly questions made us feel safe. We were learning together, and that made us relate. Even though triathlon is an individual sport, we were a team. We trained together, sweated together, and raced together, cheering for each other along the way. *Why suck at one sport when you can suck at three?* That was our training slogan.

Likewise, when I started my new life as an entrepreneur, I looked for communities where I could meet other business owners, particularly women who were also in the early days of entrepreneurship. We shared our challenges and discussed topics of interest, such as how to pitch to clients or promote our business effectively, and we ideated opportunities to collaborate, even if it was just supporting each other online, doing a podcast together, or sharing useful contacts for lawyers, accountants, and everything new founders need.

I started to have coffee chats with other entrepreneurs in Hong Kong and overseas via Zoom to brainstorm and share our experiences and challenges. Some were in very different industries, such as intellectual property, finance, or tech, but I always left feeling inspired and re-energized. Many were mums as well who, like me, were trying to juggle business and family and create a new path and a balance between both. I felt understood and supported, and many of them joined my first book signing. As part of my quest to meet other businesswomen, I joined the Women Entrepreneur Network (WEN). The organization was brilliant in welcoming both new and established businesswomen and creating a vibrant space to find inspiration, camaraderie, resources, and potential opportunities for collaboration. Listening to other womens' stories of how they were tacking obstacles and turning their ideas into a business was both inspiring and relatable. We were speaking the same language, and there was no judgment and no need for permission to be you.

Similarly, when I was trying to consolidate myself as a public speaker in 2023, I was looking for groups where I could brainstorm and connect with others in the field. Through a women's leadership summit I spoke at in Singapore that year, I discovered Keynote Women Speakers, a non-profit organization that aims to give visibility to female speakers in Asia and bridge the gender gap by promoting women in conferences and summits. I joined the organization, and through them, I met other women who were also working towards building their name and reinforcing their authority through public speaking. Although our topics of expertise were different, we connected through our vision to promote women in the public speaking space and have more representation on and off the stage.

Whether you want to start a new sport, develop a skill, or create a business, building and nurturing your tribe will help you create a peer-to-peer support network where you are there for each other, sharing learnings and resources and alleviating pain points. It's easier to find empathy in people who are going through a similar experience, and you can find ways to grow together and remove the obstacles and limiting beliefs along the way. You are not alone.

Your Mentors

The second group of people are those who are a source of inspiration. They can be mentors, peers who are ahead in their journey, or even strangers who are paving the way and show you what great looks like and how they achieve success. No matter where you are in your trajectory, there is always someone who is a few steps ahead of you. They have already cracked the beginner's code and have advanced to the next league. They can be mentors in a formal or loose sense, coaches, people you look up to, or public figures who inspire you and motivate you to push yourself to the next level.

Looking up to people helps you see what's possible and aim higher. One of my favourite creators in the personal branding space, who is now my friend, is Petra. Petra is an Austrian based in Brisbane, Australia, who has been working in strategic personal branding for eight years. She has a network of over 20,000 followers on LinkedIn and coaches top executives to build authority online through a 360 personal brand. She also has her podcast and speaks at industry events around the world. I often mention Petra as a source of inspiration because her achievements enlighten me on what's possible when you put in the effort and work hard towards your vision. Although our fields of expertise are different, and I'm focused on building my name as a public speaker and author, we share similarities in that we both leverage social media to grow and have a passion for communication, building our business online, and personal branding.

In July 2022, I connected with Petra via LinkedIn to introduce myself, and that simple message was the seed of a collaboration that then turned into a friendship. Since then, Petra and I have partnered on over twenty LinkedIn Live sessions to discuss different topics, from how to build a brand effectively to the power of book authoring to building authority and more. We even met twice in person on the Gold Coast and have built a relationship that goes beyond likes and digital platforms.

My writing mentor, Vicki, was also fundamental in my development towards becoming an author. When we first started working together in December 2022, I was a rookie in the writing world. I had only published a few dozen articles on Medium and had just finished the initial draft of my first book. I went to her with mixed feelings: I had the dream of writing and becoming an author, but having been rejected by a dozen publishers, I also had insecurities creep in. I often oscillated between feeling like an Olympian and feeling like an imposter, and she always helped me gravitate towards the Olympian. When I met her, Vicki already had a long and well-established career as an author, having published over twenty books, all with publishing houses. She was often invited to events to talk about her books and had built a name in Australia. I aspired to follow her steps and build a career as a writer, and she showed me what is possible. She, too, had started from zero and had built her success one brick at a time, or in this case, one book at a time. When I told her that I was disappointed because I hadn't found a publisher for my book and had been rejected multiple times, she smiled and said with a confident and assertive tone, 'That only means that you haven't found the perfect publisher yet.' She told me she had recently written a children's book that had been rejected and was also waiting for the perfect match. That paradigm shift helped me put things into perspective and reframe rejection into redirection.

Although Vicki was a technical mentor whose role was to help me with my writing, she also made a big impact on my mindset. I realized that I had success in me, and I had to unlock it by removing the heavy stones that were pulling me down. I always ended our calls with the confidence of a bestselling author ready to conquer the world and the enthusiasm of a child who had just learned something new. Six months later, I signed my first deal with a publishing house.

Finding mentors in life is important. They can help you face challenges and find inspiration to shape your own way of doing things and painting your canvas. Make a conscious effort to find your life mentors. Filter and be intentional about who you follow on social media, whose newsletters you read, what podcasts you listen to, and whom you seek advice from. People who walk the talk and have already been through the experience you are going through can help you have a broader perspective, avoid pitfalls, and accelerate your growth. It's easier to be great when you see what great looks like.

Your Mentees

Being someone's mentor or role model is an incredible yet often overlooked strategy to grow personally and professionally. It sounds counterintuitive at first; however, when someone comes to you for advice or sees you as a role model, you strive to give your best and live up to their expectations. It's your opportunity to own your identity and become a mentor for somebody else.

I first experienced the mentor-mentee effect when, a few months after I started writing on Medium and LinkedIn, other writers reached out to me asking for advice. Although I still considered myself a beginner, some people saw me as a reference they looked up to for starting to write online and building a personal brand from scratch. At first, I was shocked and humbled that people would see me that way. In my mind, I was still a rookie trying to figure things out in the writing scene, and although that was true, I had forgotten that in the process, I already knew much more than someone who was starting from zero.

I had several Zoom calls and interviews with other writers who had questions about my strategy and how to build an audience online across different platforms. I started to speak on podcasts with peers who wanted to learn from my experience, and every time I joined them, I tried my best to give thorough answers and illustrate my points with real examples that could help someone who was where I was six months earlier.

To this day, the imposter in me still wakes up full of energy when my name comes up as an experienced writer or an expert at anything. I'm still learning and growing, always a WIP (work in progress), but putting things in perspective is important and necessary. It helps me understand that every article I write, every newsletter I publish, and every book I launch puts me one step further.

Although you might believe that you are inexperienced, the moment you take the first step and turn an idea into action, you are one step ahead of someone else who hasn't taken that step yet. The moment you launch your website, even if it's a simple blog, you create a knowledge gap to your advantage. You can explain to someone who hasn't launched it yet why you chose one platform over another, how you decided on the layout, and what the biggest challenges were. Likewise, if you are starting a side gig, no matter how small, you can talk about the process, the business model, and your strategy to target your ideal customers. The day I did my first triathlon, I gained tons of experience that someone who had never raced yet would find invaluable.

Whenever possible, seize opportunities to become someone else's mentor and step up to the role. By sharing your experience and articulating the steps you have taken, you will reinforce your identity. Especially when you are early in your new venture, don't shy away from talking about your experience and sharing what you have learned. Many people underestimate their knowledge because they feel they are not experts or don't have enough credibility in their fields. However, sharing your learning from a place of authenticity and honesty, showing where you are and the steps and missteps you took to get there, will help attract people who want to hear from you because you have done exactly what they are trying to achieve.

Once you have your tribe with your close circle, your peers, mentors, and mentees, you have the perfect environment to create momentum. Your mentors inspire you by showing you the possibilities and what great looks like. Your peers keep you on track by raising the bar and building peer-to-peer accountability, and finally, your mentees challenge you to want to be a better role model. This is how you create an ecosystem of people where everyone grows together with an abundance mindset. It's your crew.

Summary

- If you want to make things happen, surround yourself with the right crew and build your tribe. Find people who share your goals and passions and genuinely support the identity you are trying to create.
- Change is hard, and you have to bring people on board and conquer their buy-in: share what you are doing, invite them to your backstage, give them a taste of what you are building and why it matters to you, and let them be inspired by your vision.
- Don't let the anchors hold you back. Focus your energy on your journey, your sailing, and your land. Don't expect everyone to jump on board with you, but make sure you welcome those who do with open arms. When it comes to motivation, the sum is always larger than its parts.

5

REDEFINING SUCCESS

As we saw in the first chapter, for the chain of reaction to work seamlessly, your vision must translate into results that validate your efforts and reinforce your identity. Results matter. They help you see the impact of your actions, assess the efficacy of your strategy, and course-correct when necessary. This applies to anything, whether it's learning a new skill, creating a habit, or implementing a resolution. This synergy is what keeps the chain going: Your identity manifests its vision through behaviours that lead to results, and those results invigorate your identity, reinforcing a virtuous circle of growth. You collect the fruits of your hard work; it's harvesting season.

If you aspire to be a great leader, you act as one: you listen and develop your team, take time to connect with them, and give them opportunities to grow. You prioritize their well-being and development and promote inclusion and teamwork. As a result, those reporting to you perform better and give you great feedback as a manager, reinforcing your identity as a leader. If you want to learn a new language, you take lessons and study at home. You do your homework and keep practicing. Every week, you see a slight improvement and are able to communicate a little better, a little more fluently. Your efforts pay off, and you can enjoy the reward of speaking in a foreign language.

On the other hand, when your behaviours don't translate into tangible results, your identity becomes blurry and pixelated because you don't see the correlation between what you are doing (actions and effort) and who you are becoming (identity). If your vision is to become a fit person or a great writer, you put in the hard work, expecting to see results that validate your hard work. You start going to the gym, and you write more often. You expect to look leaner or stronger and for your writing to generate more engagement, subscribers, or book sales.

Unfortunately, that math doesn't always work in practice. Very often, results are not noticeable in weeks or even months. When you are talking about major goals, it could take years. Sometimes, we even feel that we are going backwards, training, or working harder without collecting the fruits, even though it's harvesting season. Not seeing results is frustrating and can lead to a loss of confidence in the process or even in your ability to paint your canvas. If you have been going to the gym for weeks and eating healthy food, yet you fail to see any progress, you might believe that you will never be a fit person and that you are doing everything wrong. If you continue to publish articles and barely get views and reads, you might give up on your dream of being a writer because you are afraid you are not good enough. If you have been learning a language for six months and still can't follow a basic conversation, you might think you are not a language person.

Results help qualify the impact of hard work, and when you don't see them, you assume something is broken and lose motivation and faith in your new identity. Can you really be a writer, a fit person, or an entrepreneur? Insecurities creep in, and we assume the cycle is broken.

Measuring Success

It's important to find the right systems to help you measure and qualify the effectiveness of your actions so that you are headed in the right direction and progress is made, even if sometimes it's hidden from the naked eye. Some results are easier to quantify because they are concrete and specific: If you are trying to eat healthier, you can monitor your weight, fat percentage, and BMI (body mass index). If you want to become a content creator, you can measure your growth in impressions on social media and your number of subscribers. Thanks to technology, nowadays, you can measure many things: the quality of your sleep, your screen time, your weight, your sugar levels, your fitness performance, productivity, and more.

The problem is that many people look at results the wrong way in a black-or-white binary manner. They think it's about hitting one golden number: They reduce being fit to a random number on the scale, being a good writer to vanity metrics, and being successful to an arbitrary standard someone posted on social media. However, results are not the destination; your identity is. Results are tools that help you navigate towards it. If you fall into the trap of associating success with results and results with success, you will miss out on the beauty of the journey and the many stops along the way.

Outcomes are accessories: They illustrate a trend in one direction or the other, but they are not the finish line. Even if the trend is not perfectly linear and can seem flat at times, it's about connecting dots that pave the way towards your vision. Results are points in time that give you orientation and guidance, and that is what you have to focus on: the journey, the new lifestyle, the new pattern you are creating, even if, at times, the picture is blurry and the canvas is still being painted. Results in isolation are an arbitrary way to measure success that only shows one part of the picture, a distorted representation of success.

What happens when you hit a specific number of subscribers, when you receive an award as an entrepreneur or a writer, or when you finally reach a big milestone? Nothing. You celebrate the moment, and you relish your trophy, but nothing really changes. You fill your motivation jar with that token of recognition, and you keep doing what you are doing because it's cementing your identity. That particular milestone is a reward that validates what you are doing, but success is much bigger than that. It's about connecting with your purpose and loving the person you are becoming every day with your actions, your efforts, and your commitment to yourself.

Your inner validation overwrites any external award because the biggest prize is living by your life manifesto.

When an actor wins an Oscar, it's (usually) not the end of their career. Results and awards are more a recognition of their hard work and an external validation of their trajectory as a great actor rather than a closing act. Think of your tangible results as Oscars in your life cabinet and use them to motivate yourself to keep living your dream versus only chasing it. Don't fool yourself to chase a finish line: The chain of reaction is infinite and unlimited.

What happens when an article flops, you deliver a poor presentation, or spend a sedentary day at home instead of going out for a workout? Nothing. You might be disappointed, perhaps lose a business opportunity, and feel a bit flat, but that particular event in isolation doesn't change the journey and the destination. It's what you do in the long term, most days, that will have an impact on your life. Isolated results don't define your identity; they are simply tools to monitor your progress and validate that you are taking steps in the right direction.

One of my goals for 2023 was to reach 5,000 followers on Medium. I had started the year with close to 2,000 followers, and I wanted to hit a big milestone within twelve months as part of my ambition to become a writer. I published articles daily, sometimes even twice a day, and saw steady growth in my audience month after month. I was stoked. When 1 December arrived, I had reached 4,700 followers. I was so close to my target and was hoping I would hit the magic number by 31 December and celebrate the goal. I didn't. The last day of the year arrived, and I didn't hit the golden number. I was disappointed. I had not met my target, and I started to think that maybe my writing wasn't that good. Then, I reflected on it and realized that I was being unfair to myself. I was judging my success based on an arbitrary number and was letting it overwrite my efforts and my identity. I had neglected the fact that I did not have a single follower when I had started writing, and one year later, I had published over 400 articles and had almost 5,000 people who had given my writing a vote of trust. I dismissed the effort and dedication I had put into my writing for 365 days and how much confidence and skills I had developed. I disregarded the hundreds of comments I had received from readers supporting my work, adding their perspectives on my articles, or simply wanting to connect. I was building my community around writing, and slowly, my circle of influence was growing through followers, new connections, and new books. More importantly, I wasn't giving myself credit for putting in the hours of hard work and passion into something I love. I wanted to become a writer and I was living according to my life manifesto every single day. I didn't need to hit a random number to be externally validated. I was creating success with my actions. Writing consistently, persevering, and staying committed to myself was the reward. The results were just a by-product.

I was so blinded by arbitrary numbers that I was missing what was right in front of me: I had become a writer. That perspective helped me reframe the way I saw results and metrics from a destination to an accessory, the brush that helped me paint the canvas.

Dealing with Rejection

Rejection is a necessary part of the process, but it can't jeopardize your identity.

Walt Disney's first studio went bankrupt.

Einstein didn't start reading until he was seven.

Vincent Van Gogh sold one painting during his lifetime.

Stephen King had his first book, Carrie, rejected thirty times.

Henry Ford filed for bankruptcy before creating Ford Motor.

Michael Jordan was cut from his high school basketball team.

J.K. Rowling's Harry Potter was rejected twelve times by publishers.

Oprah Winfrey was fired from her first job as a TV anchor in Baltimore.

Elvis Presley was fired after his first performance at the Grand Ole Opry.

Steven Spielberg was rejected twice by the University of Southern California's School of Cinematic Arts.

If you want to quit because people told you that you are not good enough or you are not getting the results, think twice. Tell me how many times you have failed, and I will tell you how many times you will succeed.

It's easy to keep going when people praise your work, customers love your writing, and you receive stellar feedback. Humans thrive in recognition. We feel valued, appreciated, and confident. But what happens when people criticize your work, dislike your products, or even dislike you? Rejection is hard but necessary to grow, and it's critical to learn to cope with it and rise above it to keep moving forward.

My first manuscript was rejected by nineteen publishers. Every day, I have followers unfollow me, and readers unsubscribe from my newsletter. It's always a bitter experience, especially when they are paid subscribers and choose to leave after a few months. Every week, I do sales pitches to potential clients for my work as a public speaker. Around 50 per cent of my proposals are rejected or, worse, ghosted.

When I published my memoir, I had my first ever two-star rating during the launch month. There was no comment, no review, not even a title or a name. That anonymous rating devastated me, especially because it was one of the first ones and brought the rating down on Amazon. I wondered why that reader didn't bother to leave a review. I was upset. I started to visualize and anticipate many other negative reviews coming my way, and I even started to second-guess the quality of my book. It took me a few days to get over the two-star rating. After a lot of self-reflection, I embraced rejection as part of personal growth, and it's important to have self-defence mechanisms to cope with it. When I wrote about it on social media, one of my connections left an interesting comment. He said that by allowing that rating to impact my confidence and self-esteem, it was I who had rated my work a two-star without a reason. I felt uncomfortable, but he was right. I had let an arbitrary rating written by an anonymous reader impact how I saw my work. External validation is a double-edged sword and can easily turn into internal cancellation.

In many cases, we can learn from rejection. When a client gives you constructive feedback on a proposal or a project and highlights the things that could be better, you can embrace their input and improve your product or service. When readers comment on your writing, you can analyse what resonated the most and why some articles didn't land with the audience. When someone has something valuable to say, it's always worth listening with an open mind and with the intention of understanding, learning, and growing.

However, sometimes criticism comes served as a cold dish without a fork and a knife, and you have to swallow it. There is nothing you can do with it, and you know it's going to taste sour and bitter. In the digital world, this happens every day, with keyboard warriors and digital trolls. Sometimes, it's simply bored people who enjoy finding fault in others. This type of criticism is destructive and malicious, but unfortunately, the more successful you are, the more frequent it becomes.

Learning to deal with this type of negativity is crucial for your mental health and well-being and also for your motivation. Be aware of the impact it has on you and establish your own boundaries and protection layers. The more successful you are, the more immunity you will need. Personally, I know that I'm not indifferent to negativity, and it can take me into the red zone of insecurities and low self-esteem. However, I acknowledge it and rationalize the situation to stay on track. I don't engage in destructive dialogue and open negativity. Do what you need to do: delete, ignore, block, go for a walk, and find your way back into the green zone. Haters will always be haters.

Qualitative Results

A few years ago, I was at the gym with my girlfriend, Celine. We were in the changing room after a spinning class, and I commented how much fitter and toned she looked after she had started exercising a few months earlier. She nodded, saying that she was feeling much better after she had lost a couple of kilos and had more energy throughout the day. She also said that she felt more confident in the way she carried herself, and that was reflected in her attitude at work too. She was more proactive and willing to reach out to people more. Then, something happened. Before going to the showers, she stepped on the digital scale wrapped around a towel. When she saw her weight displayed on the screen, her face changed. Her smile turned into a frown, her shoulders dropped, and her energy changed in a matter of seconds. 'How did I gain one kilo?' she muttered to herself, looking down, visibly upset and disappointed. 'I thought I was doing all the right things . . .'

Even though Celine was taking all the right steps and was feeling confident, more energetic, and healthier, she had let one number define success. Just like I had done with my writing, she was reducing her identity to a metric on a scale rather than zooming out and looking at the big picture. For the previous two months, she had replaced a sedentary routine with an active lifestyle where she was walking more and hitting the gym three to four times a week; she was feeling more comfortable in front of the mirror and whenever she walked into a room; she had more energy for her children and her husband in the evenings. She spread positivity and health. She was doing all the right things. Yet, the moment she stepped on the scale, she felt like a failure because she had given an arbitrary number the power to define success, and by doing so, she had disempowered herself and discredited her hard work and erased her identity. Her chain of reaction was not broken at all; she was just looking at results the wrong way.

Success is not defined by one number at a specific point in time but by your cumulative efforts towards creating it. Humans are not machines or businesses that can be analysed with KPIs (Key Performance Indicators), profit and loss statements, and balance sheets. There are a lot of other elements, many of them intangible, that come into the equation: how you feel as a result of your actions, your level of energy, the quality of your relationships, your confidence and self-esteem, and ultimately, how happy and fulfilled you are as you start to step into your new shoes living up to your vision.

Do not step on a scale. Step into your identity.

Leading Indicators versus Lagging Indicators

When I was working at Apple, we had a leadership development session focused on leading indicators versus lagging indicators. Lagging indicators are the final outcome, the end of the equation. It could be the sales volume, your fitness level, your business growth, or any metric that measures success. Although we tend to focus on those to quantify success, we can't really affect the final outcome directly; we can only impact the factors that influence it, the leading indicators. For example, an effective marketing campaign and a higher rate of qualified leads will positively impact sales; healthy eating and regular exercise will impact your body weight and well-being; investing in media will help your business grow; hosting regular team-building activities will boost motivation, teamwork, and innovation and ultimately the team's performance. When you shift your focus and energy from lagging indicators to leading indicators, you begin to deconstruct success and assess what elements of the equation you can prioritize and invest in to impact the outcome.

Focusing on leading indicators allows you to celebrate the journey rather than obsessing about the destination and the final result. Crossing the finish line and achieving the goal is fantastic, but the little milestones along the way and the preparation to get there are equally important and fulfilling. If you let lagging indicators alone define success, you will step into an area of absolutes: black or white, success or failure, victory or loss. When you give room to leading indicators, you open the front door to your new identity: You recognize effort and progress and celebrate your chain of reaction.

Use lagging indicators and results to set the direction and use leading indicators to pave the way. Celebrate both the input and the output, the journey, and the destination.

Setting A Low Bar (and Gradually Raising It)

Countless times, I have seen people give up on their dreams because they set targets that are not realistic. They set a bar that is too high, and the result when they can't reach it is disappointment, frustration, and, ultimately, failure. I have seen it happen with entrepreneurs who give up on their start-ups, people trying to lose weight, writers giving up on their books, and individuals who stop chasing their dreams or lock them in the 'one day' high-security box, not bothering to remember where they leave the key.

'Set a high bar' has become a motivational chant productivity gurus play on repeat with conviction to an enthusiastic crowd that doesn't even know how to lift the bar. It makes you feel good; it's aspirational: you are looking up, rising like a phoenix. But like many mass motivational premises, it has loopholes and doesn't work for everyone. Sure, that approach can work for some. In his book *Can't Hurt Me: Master Your Mind and Defy the Odds*, David Goggins describes how he was so obsessed with beating the Guinness world record of push-ups in twenty-four hours that he kept going even when his hands were bleeding with excruciating blisters.

In Elon Musk's biography by Walter Isaacson, Musk said he was willing to risk everything and have his family live in a basement if that was the price to pay for reaching his ambition of sending humans to Mars. Some people are ready to remove the brakes and focus on the highest bar, the impossibly high standard people laugh about. Where there is a will, there is a way. I will challenge that by saying that where there is a will, there are many ways, and you have to find the one that works for you, staying true to who you are, your values, and your commitments and priorities.

For most, though, the concept of raising the bar high only works if you start with a low bar and continue to lift it at a pace that works for you, challenging your comfort zone. Otherwise, you will stagnate, lose confidence and momentum, and stall. Some reach the bar faster, others take longer. Some take baby steps, while others take giant steps. It does not matter. As we say in sports, 'Your race, your pace.'

That little step you think does not matter—it does. You don't go to the gym and expect to rock up with a six-pack the next day, but if you start showing up three times a week and combine it with a healthy diet, you will notice the difference after a month, and if you give consistency a vote of trust, the results after six months might be transformational. Your bar is yours for you to set, but there is one rule and one rule only: you must keep lifting it. Remember: if you are not moving up, you are falling behind. The status quo is an illusion.

In October 2003, right after finishing my master's in Madrid, I moved to Taipei, Taiwan, to do a three-month intensive course to learn Chinese. Three months is not a very long time to learn a new language, particularly if that language is very different from your mother tongue. In the case of Chinese, it's considered one of the most difficult languages in the world, and it's very different from my native language, Spanish. Mandarin has four different tones for the same sound, which means that the sound 'la' can be pronounced in four different ways, and each has a different meaning. One 'la' means pulling, while a different 'la' means spicy. On top of that, the Chinese alphabet is not based on letters, like English or French, but is built on characters, whereby each symbol has its own meaning. There are over 100,000 characters, although an educated Chinese adult knows around 8,000.

With this background, I cautiously managed my linguistic expectations. I didn't land in Taipei thinking that I was going to become fluent in Chinese in three months. Ultimately, my goal was to learn business Chinese and be able to join business meetings without a translator (high bar). However, I started by aiming to speak basic conversational Chinese (low bar) and decided not to learn the written language at first. I was only going to focus on speaking the basics to communicate with the locals and have simple conversations. I set a lower bar that was realistic and achievable, considering I was ready to study hard and put in the effort.

Setting a low bar allowed me to have a tangible objective that I knew I was capable of reaching with discipline and consistency within a reasonable time frame. Had I set a high bar and decided to become fluent in only a few months, I would have been disappointed and would probably have quit my mission, like many of my classmates did. As December arrived, my level of Mandarin was enough to have a basic conversation, order food, ask for directions on the street, and chat with people. I was over the moon to have accomplished my target and reached my bar, and that not only gave me the motivation but also the confidence to raise it a couple of inches higher. Momentum builds momentum, but more importantly, momentum builds you.

In January 2004, I moved to Shanghai to work for the Spanish Government as an intern and continued learning Chinese during lunch hours with my private tutor, Li. My new target was to speak business Chinese within a year. It was an ambitious goal, but having been able to master the basics by investing time and effort, I was ready to do the same to reach the higher bar. Li was a friendly but demanding Shanghainese teacher who came to my office three times a week during lunch hour. The sessions were always a mix of laughter and frustration. Sometimes, I wanted to burn the books and forget about the language, but at the end of each lesson, I always felt proud for having accomplished something. I then completed the homework and studied the new words before being interrogated in the next lesson. The system worked for me, and week after week, my Chinese became a little more fluent—although the frustration never went away.

When the year came to an end, I was able to accomplish things in Chinese that I once thought impossible: host business meetings, negotiate with partners and vendors, and talk about more sophisticated topics such as investment and culture. The dopamine hit from reaching the low bar was yielding motivational dividends. Feeling more confident and fluent, I raised the bar once again and decided to start learning the written form, the Chinese characters. I was already comfortable with my speaking ability (even though I still got the tones wrong), and I was keen to go up one more level and tackle the thousands of mysterious symbols. Today, I'm able to read around 3,000 characters, and I can have business conversations in Chinese and even host a presentation on topics I'm familiar with. I still take weekly lessons to maintain my fluency and learn new vocabulary. I hit my high bar, and now I keep doing repetitions to flex the muscles and keep the momentum. I started with a low bar and raised it gradually. Every time I reached the new bar, it gave me a little boost of motivation and confidence to keep going.

On the other hand, many of my classmates gave up on their targets because they raised the bar too high, mismanaging expectations. When people start learning a foreign language, they underestimate the amount of work and practice that is required to reach a conversation that allows you to follow a conversation in the way and speed at which people usually talk in the street. The learning journey usually starts with a lot of excitement and high expectations, such as, 'I want to speak fluently within a year', or 'My team speaks in French, and I want to be able to communicate with them in French.' Those are fantastic bars, but they are high, and if you don't set up realistic goals that are attainable in a relatively short time frame, you are setting yourself up for failure. It can take years to speak a language fluently, and getting the native accent is a difficult mission if you learn it as an adult. I have published three books and over 500 articles in English, have delivered dozens of presentations, workshops, and keynotes, and have never been brushed off my Spanish accent.

Understanding your current ability and what needs to be done to reach the bar is critical. Once you understand the gap and the expectations to bridge it, it's up to you to decide if you can and want to put in the effort. Most people don't fail; they quit. There is a misalignment between where they are, where they set the bar, and the work that is required to reach it. Setting the bar at the optimal level is critical to make things happen, as otherwise, not reaching it leads to disappointment, frustration, and eventually abandonment.

At the beginning of 2024, I told my husband that I wanted to learn how to do pull-ups. As a cardio fan, I have never had much upper-body strength, and I wanted to change that, not for anyone other than myself. I wanted to feel strong and powerful, and I love seeing women getting out of their comfort zone and doing things that are traditionally associated with men. They are badass, and I wanted to be badass as well. Dave is all about supporting me in whatever I want to achieve and always encourages me to make things happen. As expected, his reaction was, 'Awesome, go for it!'

One morning, we hiked up the Morning Trail, a short but steep trail walk that takes you up to the iconic Victoria Peak in Hong Kong. Our seven-year-old French bulldog, Django, was also part of the fitness squad. As we arrived at the top, we went to the fitness area, a small outdoor gym with a couple of bars and rings. Dave did his ten pull-ups in perfect shape while I watched him sitting on the floor, recovering from the sprints. When it was my turn, he said, 'Just hang from the bar straight and hold your body weight for a few seconds.'

Hesitant, I replied, 'That's it?'

'That's it,' he nodded.

I followed the instructions, and after a few seconds of hanging from the bar, I let go. I felt good. I had accomplished my task. It wasn't too hard or exhausting, but it was the first step. Next, after a short break, I focused on my first pull-up. The target was one. Not ten, not five, just one. On my first attempt, I needed to jump from the floor to get momentum so that I could lift my body up. I didn't do a real pull-up as I didn't have my head pass above my head, but I got close enough and felt great.

Two days later, I performed the same routine. I tried again, and every time, I managed to pull my body a few inches higher. After two weeks, I succeeded in doing my first pull-up. It wasn't perfect and would have disqualified me from any CrossFit event, but it was good enough to get me pumped and motivated. I slowly increased the repetitions. From one, I moved to two pull-ups while working on improving my technique. I continued lifting my low bar every week, even if it was just marginally. One day, I started trying to do the pull-up without jumping from the ground to gain momentum. It took me a few attempts, but eventually I managed. Six months later, I wasn't able to do ten, but I could do five pull-ups, which is what I do a couple of times a week. My goal is not to become a pull-up expert or compete in CrossFit games. I want to have enough muscle mass to build my core and look and feel strong. When I look in the mirror, I see more definition, and I feel strong and empowered. I'm a badass woman who can do pull-ups—even if it's only five!

It was during one of those sessions, while I was sweaty and exhausted on the floor, that I realized that the key to progress is setting your bar low, at your level, and raising it at your pace. For years, I had failed at doing pull-ups (and many other things) because I expected too much too quickly. It was only once I set a low and realistic bar that I was able to reach it, and that little win gave me the inspiration to raise it a little higher. Dream big, shoot for the stars, but set your bar low and get there first, one step at a time. Get certified in the low bar first and then fight for your promotion to the next level. It feels good, and you develop a winner's mindset.

The formula of the low bar doesn't fail: You trick your mind with tiny little wins that keep the vision alive and feed the hunger for more. Success is addictive; once you get a little taste of it, you want more. If you want to write your first book, focus on publishing your first post on social media, then go for a longer article and hone the skill. From there, you can consolidate a series of articles into an e-book and publish your first digital product. Graduate from each bar, nurture confidence, and target the slightly higher bar. Your first book starts with the first page.

The process above is the roadmap I followed to become an author and publish four books in two years. I didn't sit down one day and decide I was going to write a book. I went for the lowest common denominator of writing: a social media post. Back then, I was nowhere near ready to publish a book, but a post on LinkedIn was doable. So, I prepared a few lines and pressed the scary button to go public. Becoming active on social media was the lowest bar. It didn't demand a huge effort, but it did require a huge deal of courage: exposing yourself and your work online, something necessary for any writer.

After a couple of months of daily content creation on social media, I decided I was ready to take my bar to the next level: long articles. Long-form writing took me one step closer to writing a book, but it was within an area of comfort. I was already writing short stories, so it wasn't too daunting. I published my first articles on Medium with the same fear I had published my first posts, but slowly, the fear started to dissipate, and writing became part of my lifestyle.

Initially, my articles had little traction, and it took me a lot of effort to reach my first one hundred followers. My first month of writing generated a whoopping USD 2.15 pre-tax, and I felt like a bestselling author. If my writing was able to generate one dollar, it could certainly generate more. Slowly but surely, readers started coming, followers started to knock on my door, and after a year, I had consolidated my name on the platform. The sky was the limit! I continued doing my virtual pull-ups, flexing my writing muscles, and building confidence and competence, one article at a time. My low but always raising bar was my accomplice, the one that pushes you when you need to work harder, celebrates you when you reach your goal, and keeps you honest when your ego gets in the way. I was ready for more.

In December 2022, during my Christmas holidays in the Canary Islands, Spain, I decided I wanted 2023 to be an epic year: a year of challenges, new experiences, and personal growth. I was in proper mid-life crisis mode. I signed an accountability agreement with myself to publish my first book by 31 December 2023. The idea of raising the bar that high was intimidating, but at the same time, I had graduated from the previous level. I was starting to get too comfortable in my zone, which was the best indication that it was time to get uncomfortable.

I had no idea where to start, but I knew that I was going to make it happen. Once again, I recalibrated my bar and decided that I didn't need to write a saga or a long novel; I was going to write an actionable e-book. I was already doing a lot of writing on self-improvement, so a concise e-book was the natural evolution of my writing. I read that many e-books are 5,000 words and even shorter. *Awesome*, I thought to myself, *I can totally reach that bar.* And

I did. With my new prize in sight, I started to write my first e-book, a few pages every day. I broke it down into nineteen lessons and decided that each chapter would be around 500 to 700 words. That was totally doable. It was the equivalent of writing one article a day. Done! My chain of reaction was in motion: I had my identity (a writer), my vision (empowering people through a self-improvement book), my plan (breaking down the book into chapters), and I was executing it. It was the perfect chain, and I had to minimize resistance.

I dedicated around two hours to writing my book every day, and in one month, I had the very first draft, far from ready but far from nothing. I had just hit the second milestone. The first one was writing the first page, and taking the first step. For the first time in my life, I felt what the compound effect meant as a writer. I had experienced it before, whether it was with the stocks, learning languages, or exercising. High effort always yielded incremental dividends over time. The compound effect had always been a constant in my life, whether it was learning a new skill or getting things done, but for the first time, I tasted it in the writers' world. Those seemingly unimportant two hours that I was spending every day running miles on my keyboard were now coming together under the shape of a book, my first book. When I finished the last page, I checked the word count, and it was 12,000. It was way less than the average book, which has around 50,000 words, but way more than the short e-books of 5,000 that I had targeted as a starting point. I was happy with that. I had a raw diamond ready to be polished. I had reached my bar and was ready to move up a level.

Once you build momentum, you just have to let things flow, follow the gentle current, and remove resistance and obstacles along the way. Just keep doing what you are doing. Dedicate a couple of hours a day to your project. It doesn't have to be five hours. Keep the flow alive. Take breaks and let your mind recover, but don't slack. It's easy to keep going when you are going, but it's hard to restart the engine after you let it cool down for too long. Don't hibernate, recalibrate. Don't pull the brake; take a break. We build momentum as much as momentum builds us: Once things are in motion, we start to believe in ourselves. Action makes us believe, and belief is fuel for action. Don't break the virtuous cycle; feed the chain of reaction, nurture it, and keep the ball rolling.

After the first draft, all engines were on, and there was no slowing down, partly because I could start to see the finish line and partly because I believed in myself. I was making it happen, and there was little resistance because the elements of the chain of reaction were in sync. In February 2023, three months after I sat down to write the first page, *The Lemon Tree Mindset* was listed on Amazon as an e-book. Two months later, I published its paperback edition. I ordered the author's copy, and for the first time in my life, I was reading a book both as its reader and its author. That thin booklet with a bright yellow lemon tree on the cover was insignificant in the ocean of books.

On launch day, it ranked 2,133,548 on Amazon. But that same little book had a huge impact on my life: It was the authenticity stamp that sealed my identity as a writer and an author. Regardless of the book sales or the ranking, it was a critical step in my chain of reaction. I had started with my (aspirational) identity, had set my low bar, and, day after day, had lifted it just a little, but enough to keep me going up. That little step that I thought did not matter, did. It was the compound effect of betting on my dream and of betting on myself. Some call it a crazy bet; I call it the safest bet of all. You can only ever win.

Find Your Win

No matter what you want to do in life, a winner's mindset helps you accomplish it. However, a winner's mindset is not about winning all the time and collecting gold medals, it's about finding the win in every situation and always bringing home a participant medal, even if you came last in the race.

It's up to you to find success in what you do every day, not only in the fruits you collect and the results you produce. You are the ultimate judge of your actions and your impact. Whether you see the outcome as a success or as a failure depends on the perspective you use and the lenses you adopt. Don't focus only on the tree. Celebrate the tiny seed as well because planting it is the only way you will ever have not one but many trees.

Some days, you will have big wins, hit milestones, win races, gain clients, deliver great services, and climb on the podium. These are the days that give you confidence and fire you up to keep going. You want to high-five yourself, and the sky is the limit. On other days, it's the polar opposite. Deals fall through, your run is slow, people unfollow you, you miss your workout, you face writer's block, and things just don't seem to flow. We all have those days, and they open the door to distraction, temptation, and abandonment. If you don't see results anyway, you might as well go back to your old self and eat poorly, browse endlessly through social media, and give up on the article you were working on.

Every day, every experience, every situation is an opportunity for a win, however small. Try to find one thing worth celebrating. When I launched my newsletter, I celebrated every single new subscription. The problem is, some days, I had none. Those days, I forced myself to find something else worth appreciating. Perhaps I made a slight improvement on the design, learned something new about the platform, or had a great connection with someone new. It didn't matter what I was celebrating. I was creating my win, and by doing that, I was developing a winner's mindset.

In January 2024, I ran the Hong Kong Standard Chartered Half Marathon. I hadn't been able to train properly during the Christmas holidays in Spain, and my preparation had been far from ideal. The week before the race, I told Dave I was not going to participate because I didn't feel ready and I was going to be slow anyway. 'What's the point?' I whispered. Surprised, Dave looked at me and objected, 'You absolutely have to run it. It doesn't matter if your running time is slow. Every time you finish a race and cross the finish line, you feel amazing afterwards, and it will challenge you and inspire you to reach your next target. Just do it. That's you and what you love doing regardless of your time.'

He was 100 per cent right. That was me! On Sunday, 21 January, I woke up at 5 a.m. I prepared my race bag, had my coffee and a quick breakfast, and walked out of the door in the dark. The moment I headed towards the Kennedy Town subway station wearing my participant dorsal, the reality of race day started to sink in. I had butterflies in my stomach; I was earning my identity of being a fit mum who loves exercising and setting a role model for my daughters. I was living my vision, and that filled me with purpose and passion.

I arrived at the starting point and was surrounded by thousands of strangers who had taken over the Tsim Sha Tsui district. I could feel the frantic energy of the crowds and the nerves in the air. When the marshal's gun went off at 7.40 a.m., I started my 21-kilometre run, in the city I love, the place that has been home for the past seventeen years. From the beginning, I was slower than my average pace and couldn't keep up with the pacer I had targeted, but I kept running. Many participants passed me along the way, and I had moments of darkness, but I kept running, one step at a time. 'Your race, your pace,' I kept telling myself. The music and the spectators cheering gave me goosebumps and extra fuel for my legs. I faced my demons and reminded myself of how lucky I was to be there, doing what I love, supported by the people I love. My tribe.

When I reached the final corridor, with the finish line in sight, I could see the time: 1 hour 52 minutes. It was much slower than any of my times in previous years. However, it didn't matter. I sprinted with the energy I had left, smiling and high-fiving the spectators on the sides. I finished the run with a huge sense of accomplishment, and when I received my participant medal, I kissed it with a proud smile. I had pushed myself, fought resistance, and achieved something. Instead of being disappointed or letting a random number on a digital screen define success for me, I redefined it. I had found my win in showing up and living according to my values.

There is no such thing as failure if you decide to learn from it and turn it into an opportunity. A win is not necessarily winning a deal, clocking a personal best (PB) at a race, or selling more books. A win can also be a lesson, a learning, or a new experience. It's up to you to find it and embrace it. Zoom out and look at the big picture of the identity you are working towards. If you aspire to become a successful entrepreneur, a win can be a great conversation with a potential client (even if you didn't close the deal), completing a course online about entrepreneurship, or joining a network to build your community. Although these are not considered results, they are certainly actions that help you consolidate your identity. I remember the day I printed my first business cards as an entrepreneur. I was over the moon; it reaffirmed my dream.

Embracing the small wins and finding the lessons in the failures, the losses, and the mistakes help you nurture a positive and growth mindset. Every day, you have an opportunity to do something that reinforces your vision, and that little step is worth celebrating. To this day, I carry the tradition of sharing the wins of the day with my husband in the evening. We always have a chat about what happened, the highlights of the day, the girls' stories, and then we share big things and little things worth celebrating.

One day, I was devastated because I had lost a deal with a client I looked forward to working with as a public speaker. It was a world-class sports brand, and I was the candidate shortlisted to deliver a keynote at their regional event in Hong Kong. After I sent them a quotation for my session, they replied, saying that they had decided to go for another speaker because my fee was too high. I was extremely disappointed initially, but after processing the feelings of rejection, I realized that it had been a huge entrepreneurship lesson. I learned that I hadn't been able to show and articulate my value clearly. I had sent them a proposal without a discovery call because they were in a rush, and I gave them my standard quotation. I had become one more vendor for them and had entered the price battle. After they rejected my offer, I realized that I had missed an opportunity to explain more effectively the value I could add with my experience combining leadership, culture, and sports. I had rushed the process. I didn't mention that I customize the content to align with their company values and language. I didn't pause to seek more information about their needs before offering a solution. I had lost a deal, but I had learned a lesson and a powerful one, and a lesson is always a win.

Eventually, after the event, I contacted the organization again and asked to have a meeting in person to build the relationship and understand more about their training needs and plans in the region. I went to their office in Hong Kong and had a great conversation with their Diversity, Equity, and Inclusion team. I asked them about their strategy for people development and their key challenges, and I talked about my experience supporting organizations through workshops and team-building activities. We had a great connection, and although nothing came out of that particular meeting, they then referred me to their HR team, who, five months later, selected me to speak at one of their events. I turned the loss into a win and the no into a yes. That was my win for the day.

You can always find your win. When your chain of reaction is aligned, so are you. You feel connected to your purpose and validated by your actions, regardless of the outcome and the results. You celebrate the effort and the road less travelled with all its hardship and its peaks. You appreciate the journey and its many stops along the way. What would be the point of winning a race you didn't train hard for? Is there a true reward without effort? The biggest win is not the score. It's taking part in the game, your game, and bringing home the participant medal you earned with your sweat.

Summary

- Success is non-binary: it's not dictated by arbitrary numbers and milestones but by living with purpose, in alignment with your identity and your values.
- Results are tools and points in time, but the true reward lies in living intentionally and working towards a better version of yourself with effort and commitment. You can only truly embrace growth when you embrace rejection as part of the journey because it makes you appreciate it even more.

- When you become the main character in the life you want to live, you really don't care about the result. You care about showing up knowing there's no other place where you would rather be than right here, painting your colourful canvas.

YOUR STORY

This book has hopefully taken you on a journey during which you have discovered more about yourself, your identity, your default mindset, and your blind spots.

Everything starts with you: your vision and your identity, an ever-evolving unapologetic version of yourself. Every one of us is different, but we all have greatness and potential in us to activate our chain of reaction and lift the anchors along the way to navigate and reach our life goals.

There will always be resistance along the way. We are wired to follow our primitive instincts and favour pleasure over effort and relief over discomfort. Humans are procrastinators by nature and anti-procrastinators by choice. Your choice.

Once you know yourself, once you really know yourself, it all goes down to the thousands of conscious and deliberate choices you make every day. You can decide to be in the green zone and nurture a space for productivity and infinite growth. You can be proactive and seal the cracks before procrastination sneaks in. You can surround yourself with a tribe of people who lift you up and inspire you to be better, and in the process, you will inspire those around you too. In every situation, you can find your win.

Lift your anchors and keep sailing.